Peruvian Wildlife

A VISITOR'S GUIDE TO
THE CENTRAL ANDES

Barry Walker
Huw Lloyd
with
Gerard Cheshire

edition

www.bradtguides.com

Bradt Travel Guides Ltd, UK
The Globe Pequot Press Inc, USA

First published November 2007

Bradt Travel Guides Ltd
23 High Street, Chalfont St Peter, Bucks SL9 9QE, England
www.bradtguides.com
Published in the USA by The Globe Pequot Press Inc,
246 Goose Lane, PO Box 480, Guilford, Connecticut 06437-0480

Text copyright © 2007 Barry Walker, Huw Lloyd and Gerard Cheshire
Maps copyright © 2007 Bradt Travel Guides Ltd
Illustrations © 2007 Individual photographers and artists (see below)
Series Editor: Mike Unwin

British Library Cataloguing in Publication Data
A catalogue record for this book is available from the British Library

ISBN-10: 1 84162 167 6
ISBN-13: 978 1 84162 167 8

Photographs
Heather Angel/Natural Visions (HA/NV), Arco Images/Alamy (AI/A),
Blickwinkel/Alamy (B/A), Rick & Nora Bowers/Alamy (RNB/A),
Amazon- Images/Alamy (AI/A), Konrad Zelazowski/Alamy (KZ/A),
Edward Parker/Alamy (EP/A), Stock Connection Distribution/Alamy (SCD/A),
Danita Delimont/Alamy (DD/A), Mylene d'Auriol (MDA), Aaron Boyd (AB),
Hilary Bradt (HB), James Brunker (JB), Pablo Goncalves (PG),
Paul Hakimata/Dreamstime (PH/A), Anthony Lujan (Al), Jeffrey S Pippen (JSP),
Heinz Plenge (HP), James Preston (JP), Pete Oxford (PO), Manzanita Project (MP),
Peter Price (PP), Nick Richter (NR), Forest & Kim Starr (FKS), Nicole Tharp (NT),
Tony Morrison/South American Pictures (TM/SAP), Nicole Tharp (NT),
Alan Watson/Forest Light (AW/FL), Rob Williams (RW)
Title page Spectacled bear (JS) Inca orchid (HP) Leaf iguana (HP)

Illustrations Gerard Cheshire
Maps Malcolm Barnes

Designed and formatted by Pepenbury Ltd
Printed and bound in India at Ajanta Offset & Packagings Ltd, New Delhi

CONTENTS

Box features

ACKNOWLEDGEMENTS

Barry Walker is indebted to the following: his wife Charo and daughter Alicia for support on this project; the late Ted Parker who helped him along in the early days and Huw Lloyd who agreed to be co-author of the guide

Huw Lloyd is indebted to the following people: his brother Andrew and his family; his parents Hilda and Malcolm; his late grandfather, Walter, for buying him his first ever pair of binoculars; Stuart Marsden; Eliana Manga; all the staff at Manu Expeditions; Gerri Thomas, his birding mentor in South Wales; Arthur Morgan and Brian Cox, his most inspirational teachers; and all his fellow post-graduate sufferers at the EGS department, Manchester Metropolitan University.

Thanks also to David Hilton for his notes on the *Seven of the best* chapter.

AUTHORS

Barry Walker was born near Manchester, England, and started bird watching at the age of 13. After first pursuing this interest all over Europe and the Middle East, he switched his attention to the Neotropics and has since gained extensive birding experience in Chile, Ecuador, Colombia, Brazil, Bolivia and – especially – Peru, where he has now lived for over 25 years. Barry has participated in many ornithological expeditions and contributed to many publications concerning Peruvian birds, and is the author of the well received book *A Field Guide to the Birds of Machu Picchu and the Cuzco area, Peru*. He has also visited every corner of the country as a trekking and natural history guide, and has been leading bird tours for private groups and bird tour companies for the last 15 years. Barry lives in Cusco and is married with a 10-year-old daughter. His wife Rosario is owner of Manu Expeditions, a pioneer eco-tour operator in Manu specializing in natural history, horse riding and cultural trips. Barry also occupies the post of British Consul in Cusco and received an MBE in the 2004 Queen's New Years Honours lis.

Huw Lloyd currently lives in Manchester, England, and has been leading bird-watching tours throughout Peru since 2000. He was born in South Wales and began birding at the age of 11 with the local branch of the Young Ornithologists Club. His interest in tropical birds began when he participated in the Manchester Metropolitan University expedition to Sumba Island, Indonesia – winner of the 1993 BirdLife International-BP Conservation expedition award. Since 1995 he has been studying the ecology of Peruvian birds, completing a number of research programmes on threatened forest bird communities. He lived in southeast Peru for two years and in 1999 worked for the Duke University tropical ecology field programme in Costa Rica. He is currently completing his doctorate thesis on the ecology and conservation of globally threatened Polylepis birds in Peru and is a member of the ornithological research committee for the Peruvian non-governmental organization Asociación Ecosistemas Andinos. He is also a regular consultant for the globally-threatened bird species programme (Peru) with BirdLife International.

Gerard Cheshire spent his formative years living near the New Forest in England, where he developed an early enthusiasm for natural history. Having become a Bachelor of Science at University College London he decided to utilise his extensive knowledge of fauna and flora by cultivating a career as a freelance author. He has now been writing about wildlife for over ten years and become well established in this field. He lives in Bath with his wife and three sons.

PRINCIPAL PHOTOGRAPHER

Heinz Plenge (*www.plenge.com*) is a wildlife photographer and conservationist who works with local communities helping them protect and benefit from their natural resources. His photos have been published worldwide in books and magazines including *National Geographic*, *GEO*, *BBC Wildlife*, *Natural History* and *WWF Magazine*. He has published nine books. Currently, he divides his time between his photographic activities and his administration of the Chaparri Ecological Reserve in Peru.

Cloud forest (HP)

HOW TO USE THIS BOOK

Due to the prolific biodiversity of the Peruvian Andes it is impossible in a book of this size to do justice to everything. Our main aim, therefore, is to present a balanced and colourful overview of the region's wildlife from a visitor's perspective. Readers with a more specific interest, such as butterflies or birds, are encouraged to use the relevant field guides to find out more. See *further reading* page 140.

The major taxonomic groups that you are likely to encounter are described here in separate sections. We do not concentrate on wildlife identification per se, but each section introduces key plants and animals, and describes some of the more interesting ecological, behavioural and – in some cases – cultural aspects of those species. Our selection of species reflects those that are most typical of the Peruvian Andes, and that are either unique to or highly threatened in the region; in other words, those that the average visitor is most keen to see and most likely to encounter.

We have attempted to make the taxonomy as reader-friendly as possible by providing common (English) or local (Peruvian/Spanish) names where possible. However, there are a number of species groups, particularly amongst the plants, reptiles and amphibians, that do not have handy common names. Therefore, we feel that a basic grasp of taxonomic terminology is helpful, as in the two following examples:

	Spectacled bear	**Golden-headed quetzal**
Kingdom	Animalia (animals)	Animalia (animals)
Phylum	Chordata (vertebrates)	Chordata (vertebrates)
Class	Mammalia (mammals)	Aves (birds)
Order	Carnivora (carnivores)	Trogoniformes (near-passerines)
Family	Ursidae (bears)	Trogonidae (trogons)
Genus	*Tremarctos* (tremarctine bears)	*Pharomachrus* (quetzals)
Species	*Tremarctos ornatus* (spectacled bear)	*Pharomachrus auriceps* (golden-headed quetzal)

The *Introduction* gives some background to the Peruvian Andean environment, including its geology, topography, biogeography and climate. It also describes the major habitat types, with some notes on associated microhabitats and the dominant plant species of each habitat. The *Where to go* chapter describes key conservation areas and wildlife destinations, as well as offering tips on travel, watching wildlife and photography. Other chapters are broadly arranged around the major groups into which plants and animals are classified, with boxes used to highlight topics of particular interest to the traveller.

INTRODUCTION

THE PERUVIAN ANDES: A HOTSPOT OF BIODIVERSITY

The tropical Andes have been described as the richest and most diverse of the world's 34 biodiversity hotspots, with around 15,000 endemic plants, and nearly 500 threatened species of amphibian, bird and mammal. And it is in Peru, home to some of the most impressive mountain scenery on earth, that the Andes are at their richest. Only here can you travel from high altiplano steppe down to pristine Amazonian rainforest in one continuous, unbroken journey, or descend from humid elfin forests directly into the spectacular desert canyon of the Marañón Valley. Nowhere else on earth can you spend days hiking through deep glacial valleys, dwarfed by snow-capped peaks of over 6,000m, and explore some of the world's largest remaining tracts of rare *Polylepis* woodland.

A fairly reliable tourist and transport infrastructure means that the Peruvian Andes are among the most accessible mountains in South America. Consequently, travellers can experience Andean wildlife in Peru more easily than anywhere else in South America. With very little effort, the national bird of Peru – the Andean cock-of-the-rock – can be seen daily strutting and scrambling at regular display grounds in the lush cloud forests of Manu National Park. Butterfly enthusiasts will be in seventh heaven at the sheer volume and diversity around Machu Picchu. And the humid forests of southern Peru are some of the best places to see spectacled bears and large troops of the common woolly monkey.

Peru is often referred to as the 'Land of the Incas'. While the Incas undoubtedly represented one of the greatest empires in the history of South America, creating

Cordillera blanca: the highest mountain range in the tropics (HB)

Clumps of puna grass with El Misti volcano in the background (TM/SAP)

archaeological wonders such as the cities of Choquequirau and Machu Picchu, they were actually the last in a long series of Andean civilisations spanning thousands of years. Many ruins and other archaeological sites belonging to the Chavin, Moche or Wari cultures can still be seen today in many locations in central and southern Peru.

Today the Peruvian Andes are home to millions of indigenous highland people, who still speak in their traditional languages of Quechua and Aymara. While many of the larger Andean cities preserve the legacy of the Spanish conquests, many smaller towns and villages maintain their traditional way of life. Journeying through Peru, the traveller will frequently pass through extensive areas of agriculture and hills that have been farmed in similar fashion for thousands of years. In many areas of southern Peru, Andean communities maintain a strong sense of their cultural identity by wearing their distinctive ponchos, with each design and combination of colours unique to their community or region.

The human impact on wildlife and natural habitats has been quite severe in the tropical Andes, particularly on the humid montane forests. In some areas of Peru, the continued loss and degradation of these forests is of great international concern because of the threat it poses to their many endemic species. Consequently the distribution of many endemic Andean species is now highly fragmented and their populations are inadequately protected. Responsible ecotourism to Peru helps promote global awareness of the plight of threatened Andean wildlife and actively contributes toward its conservation. This book aims to show how responsible visitors can experience the wonder of seeing these species in their natural habitats, and also to highlight some of the conservation successes achieved by the Peruvian authorities.

GEOLOGY

The Andes range is the longest continuous mountain chain in the world, stretching more than 7,000km (4,400 miles) along the western edge of South America. The mountains were created by the process known as continental drift. Put simply, the earth's crust comprises a number of large sections known as tectonic plates that fit together like the pieces of a giant jigsaw puzzle. These are not fixed in position. Instead, they float on a universal ocean of molten, fluid rock called magma, so that convection currents generated beneath the crust push and pull them about. In places where tectonic plates are being pulled apart, magma wells up into the gap and solidifies to form new crust. In places where they are being forced together, two things can happen: either one plate slips below the other to form a subduction zone, or the plates crumple up to form mountain ranges. The Andes are the result of two tectonic plates being pushed together for millions of years, with the fault line running offshore, parallel with the Pacific coast of South America.

In geological terms the Andes are relatively young, having begun their formation during the late Tertiary period, about 20 million years ago. The mountains are thus still developing, but their growth is perpetually held in check by the processes of erosion. Huascarán, at 6,768m above sea level, is Peru's highest mountain, and the second highest in South America after Argentina's Aconcagua (6,962m). Glacial movements and freeze–thaw action erode the exposed rock at high altitude, while running water continues the process lower down, so that streams and rivers cut and carry away debris in an ongoing process. The mountains are studded with volcanoes,

The shadow of the Ausangate Cordillera mountain range reflects in the still lake waters (HP)

formed by magma that – under enormous pressure from the offshore subduction zone – burst upwards through faults and fissures and spewed out onto the surface. Many of these volcanoes are extinct, but there are still plenty of active ones.

Among the igneous rocks (those of volcanic origin) that make up the Andes are also ancient sedimentary rocks such as sandstone, mudstone and limestone that were deposited before the mountains rose from the earth's crust. These contain many fossils that betray the natural history of the continent in primordial times. Indeed, fossils found in the Andes by Charles Darwin helped him formulate his theory of evolution.

In cross-section from east to west the Southern Peruvian Andes have a distinctive profile. In effect there are two mountain ranges running alongside one another, with a high altitude plain or steppe – the *altiplano* – lying between. Further north the cross section has deep valleys and more ranges. The mountain slopes to the east have been heavily eroded by water, which has carried their material down to the Amazon Basin along the tributaries of the great river. This has left them jagged and precipitous, with sharp ridges rising between steep valleys. The slopes to the west are very different. They have suffered comparatively little from erosion, due to the scarcity of water, so the terrain slopes away far more gently and evenly. The foothills to the east fall from cloud forest into rainforest, while those to the west carry the sands of semi-desert and desert.

EVOLUTION AND BIODIVERSITY

South America's complex biogeographical history is reflected in today's fauna and flora. The continent started life conjoined with other continents in a 'megacontinent' called Pangaea. It thus shared a universal fauna and flora with the rest of the world, which lasted until the Triassic period approximately 250 million years ago, when reptiles were the dominant animals and gymnosperms the most advanced plants. Pangaea then began gradually to divide into two super-continents, Laurasia in the northern hemisphere and Gondwana in the southern hemisphere. This occurred over the Jurassic and Cretaceous periods, which saw first dinosaurs, then flowering plants and finally marsupial mammals appear. Laurasia and Gondwana eventually separated completely, so that marsupial mammals dominated the southern super-continent, while placental mammals prevailed on the northern super-continent. Australia then broke away, while the rest of Gondwana (South America and Africa) rejoined with Laurasia, allowing placental mammals to migrate south, and seeing the ancestors of such mammals as camelids and primates evolve. Shortly afterwards South America was set adrift by the formation of the Atlantic Ocean. Eventually it became connected once again with North America, so that very different plants and animals were able to spill across in both directions. At about the same time, the formation of the Andes produced a temperate climate at higher altitudes, allowing Laurasian plants and animals to find a new foothold.

Since then, the equatorial lowlands of Peru have become dominated by tropical and semi-tropical plants and animals, while the mountains have continued to harbour relict populations whose lineage stems from the northern hemisphere.

Consequently, the Peruvian Andes are a veritable cornucopia of species. In fact, scientists have calculated that Peru probably has more species of both plant and animal than any other country, even though, at 1,285,200km², it comes only nineteenth in terms of land area. To put things in perspective, the Russian Federation is thirteen times bigger than Peru, while the USA is nearly eight times the size.

CLIMATE

The wide spectrum of plants and animals in the Peruvian Andes owes much to the variety of habitats. This, in turn, is significantly influenced by climate. The topography of the mountains means that the eastern flank receives plenty of rainfall, while the western flank suffers a dearth. The reasons for this are the markedly different influences of the Pacific Ocean to the west and the Amazon Basin to the east. The effect of this polarity over time has been heavy erosion on the eastern slopes and an accumulation of material on the western slopes. This has influenced the soil, so that the eastern slopes have a covering of mostly sedimentary materials, mixed with varying levels of humus and detritus from decomposed organisms. By contrast, the western slopes, where most of the organic material is blown away, are covered with dry sands and gravels. Consequently, the eastern slopes are fertile and life-giving, while the western slopes are relatively infertile and barren. Put simply, there are forests to the east and deserts to the west!

Another critical influencing factor on plant life, and consequently animal life, is the temperature, which varies by about 0.6°C per 100m of altitude. Weather systems in the southern hemisphere move from east to west across the Amazon rainforest, picking up moisture from the humid environment as they go. On reaching the Andes the humid air rises and is cooled and the terrain becomes blanketed in clouds and mist for much of the time – hence the cloud forest. Even during the distinct dry season from May to September, the cloud forest interior above 2,000m remains cool and moist. High in the Andes above 4,000m conditions are very different, with intense solar radiation by day and biting frost at night.

HABITATS

This section describes the general Andean habitats of Peru that you are likely to encounter on your travels. For the sake of simplicity, they are categorised into main habitats, only mentioning a number of associated microhabitats in passing.

ALTIPLANO STEPPE (ALPINE ZONE)

On top of the Andes, on slopes above 5,000m in elevation, is an environment known as the altiplano steppe, or alpine zone, which comprises a number of very particular habitats, including glaciers, glacial rivers and boulder scree. Many are mostly devoid of vegetation, instead forming stretches of cold, barren desert and alkaline lakes. Very few plants and animals inhabit this harsh environment. Those that do, such as the rosette herb *Stangea erikae* (Erika's valerian) in central Peru, grow in tight groups, close to the ground, and exhibit specialised alpine characteristics such as rounded, succulent, overlapping leaves to cope with the extreme conditions.

The sweeping puna grasslands with the Vilcanota range in the background. (TM/SAP)

PUNA GRASSLAND

Puna grassland is semi-humid grassland, either of pure grass or mixed with scattered shrubs. It occurs above the humid cloud and elfin forest habitats (see below) and covers the Andean slopes above 4,000m in elevation from northern-central Peru all the way to the south of the country. The dominant vegetation is coarse bunch grasses, in particular *Festuca* and *Calamagrostis* species, often mixed with *Baccharis* and *Senecio* shrubs. There are also frost-resistant cushion plants such as *Distichia* and *Oxychloë*, and several *Tephrocactus* cacti species.

PARAMO GRASSLAND

Paramo grassland is more humid and mixed, with shrubby vegetation. It replaces the drier puna vegetation in areas of central and northern Peru, and is often dominated by plants from the Compositae family, such as *Espeletia*, which are related to sunflowers. Typical grass species are *Agrostis* (bent-grasses) and *Stipa* (sedge-grasses), and there are also ferns (*Blechnum* spp.) and terrestrial bromeliads (*Puya* spp.).

AQUATIC ENVIRONMENTS

Thousands of freshwater lakes are dotted around the puna and paramo. The two most famous are also the largest, Lake Titicaca and Lake Junín. Lake Titicaca is situated on the Peru–Bolivia border and is the largest lake in the world above 3,800m. The meaning of its name has been obscured by the passage of time. Some scholars believe it to have meant 'rock of the puma' (referring to Titicaca island), while others feel that 'crag of lead' seems more likely. Either way, the lake covers an area of 8,562km² (about the same size as Corsica) and reaches a depth of 284m, with

Lake Titicaca (RW)

a total capacity of about 800km³. Despite being officially classified as a freshwater lake, Titicaca has a salinity level of 0.78–1.2 grams per litre (or parts per thousand), making it slightly brackish (sea water is about 3.5 grams per litre). Mineral salts and other soluble minerals from the eroding rocks of the surrounding mountains are responsible for this, being carried to the lake in ground water.

Lake Junín (known locally as *Chinchaycocha*) is the second highest lake in Peru, at 4,082m. Although it covers an area of over 40,000ha, the lake itself is fairly shallow, reaching depths of only 12.5m. It is home to numerous endemic flora and fauna, and is officially designated as the Junín National Reserve and as a Ramsar wetlands site of international importance.

Andean bogs are perennially wet, with a constant supply of water from glacial run-off. They are often situated on poorly drained, gravelly or sandy soils, with a deep organic layer of peat. The dominant plant species are tuft-forming grasses and *Bryidae* mosses.

SCRUB

Scrub takes different forms in the Andes, again depending on altitude. Arid montane scrub is characteristic of the drier inter-montane valleys of the Peruvian Andes above 2,700m. It grows on rocky slopes, and comprises a variety of smaller trees, woody shrubs, terrestrial bromeliads and cacti. Semi-humid montane scrub is a denser, shrubbier habitat found especially in the moist inter-montane valleys of the Peruvian Andes at 2,500–4,000m, which often act as an 'elevational corridor' between higher and lower habitats. It is dominated by small trees such as *Schinus* and *Caesalpinia*, and plants such as *Baccharis*, *Eupatorium*, *Berberis*, *Lupinus* and *Hesperomeles*. Much of this habitat is highly degraded, making it one of the most threatened habitats in the Peruvian Andes.

Polylepis woodland (HB)

ELFIN FOREST

The Andes has a variety of forest and woodland habitats that, again, are largely determined by the altitude at which they grow. Elfin forests are stunted, evergreen forests found at the natural treeline, below the grasslands, on the humid eastern slopes of the Andes. The trees are often flat-topped in shape, from prolonged exposure to strong winds, giving the forests a sculptured appearance. Elfin forests occur at elevations of 2,800–3,600m, and are dominated by plant genera such as *Clusia*, *Gynoxys*, *Miconia*, *Escallonia* and *Weinmannia*. Bamboo (*Chusquea*) and tree ferns (*Cyathea*) are also characteristic features of this zone.

CLOUD FOREST

Cloud forest forms the largest extent of woodland along the eastern slope of the Peruvian Andes. It is generally found at 900–3,000m, although the exact elevation varies from region to region and depends on the height at which clouds most frequently come into contact with the mountains – thus providing the forests with their essential moisture. The largest trees have compact crowns, with many thick, twisted branches. They attain a height of 25–30m and many are covered in mosses and lush epiphytes. Common cloud forest plant genera include *Brunellia*, *Oreopanax*, *Podocarpus*, *Prunus* and *Alnus*. Tree ferns and highland palm species are also conspicuous members of this plant community.

POLYLEPIS WOODLAND

Polylepis woodland is a high-altitude Andean forest habitat that occurs at elevations of 3,500–5,000m – much higher than the more humid cloud and elfin forests. It is surrounded by paramo or puna grasslands and shrub communities, and consists mainly of evergreen trees of the genus *Polylepis* (Rosaceae), which are highly drought tolerant. The trunk and branches of these trees are laminated with brown-reddish bark that peels off in paper-like sheets as protection against extremely low temperatures.

Columnar torch cactus grows on the arid western slope of the Andes. (HP)

DESERT

The western flank of the Peruvian Andes is an arid strip of semi-desert and desert habitat that continues down to the Pacific coast and extends from the coast some 20–100km inland to the secondary ridges of the Andes (up to 3,200m elevation). It covers an area of almost 189,000km², extending from southern Peru to the country's northernmost limit near the city of Piura. From December to March, conditions are extremely hot and sunny, with temperatures ranging from 25°–38°C. From June to September, it is significantly cooler and more cloudy, with temperatures varying from 16°C at night to 24°C during the day. Like most deserts, the Sechura is characterised by scant plant cover. However, a number of species are found on the arid, rocky western Andean slopes, most noticeably various species of cacti, such as the Peruvian torch cactus (*Echinopsis peruviana*).

THE FORESTS OF MACHU PICCHU

The forest structure on the eastern slope of the Andes gradually changes from the lowlands to the highlands. This is well illustrated at Peru's best-known tourist destination, the world famous Machu Picchu Historical Sanctuary. At 2,000m, trees are 20–30m tall, as can be seen in the Mandor Valley. Their trunks are often straight and smooth, and fast-growing pioneer *Cecropia* trees, with their large silvery leaves,

 are common. Above this altitude, the forest becomes lower and impenetrable, the gnarled trunks festooned with epiphytes, including mosses, lichens, ferns, orchids and bromeliads. Even higher, at around 3,200m, the elfin forest is more stunted, with dense, leathery-leaved trees draped in lichens and moss. These shiny leaves condense moisture into droplets that form the characteristic mist in these areas and are an important source of moisture in the dry season. Higher still, above 3,800m, are the fragments of *Polylepis* woodland, with their characteristic shining leaves and peeling bark. The *Polylepis* woodlands at Machu Picchu are very important, since elsewhere in South America this habitat is under intense pressure from overgrazing, burning and the harvesting of firewood. Above the treeline lies the humid paramo, with its spongy mix of small bushes, tall grass and mosses. In drier areas this is replaced by uniform puna grassland. Above 4,400m the vegetation becomes very sparse, comprising mainly rosettes and cushion plants that can tolerate the intense solar radiation, frost and snow that come at this altitude. Glaciers start at 5,000m, though these are now noticeably retreating.

PLANTS

Sobralia dichotoma (HP)

This section aims to introduce some of the most common, historically significant and remarkable plants of the Peruvian Andes. Many can easily be found among Peru's historic landmarks and protected areas. Peru has a special significance for the conservation of Andean flora because of its variations in altitude and climate, and its wide range of habitats and microhabitats. These factors have led to the evolution of many endemic species.

ANGIOSPERMS (FLOWERING PLANTS)

The angiosperms, or flowering plants, are the dominant group in the plant kingdom and were the last major group of plants to evolve, emerging during the Jurassic period and diversifying rapidly during the Cretaceous period. They comprise

grasses, herbaceous plants, shrubs and most trees. In angiosperms, the seed embryo (angiosperm) is enclosed, so the pollen has to grow a tube to penetrate the protective seed coat. This account focuses on some of the more interesting or conspicuous varieties that you are likely to encounter.

Angiosperms are broadly divided into two types: monocotyledons (monocots) and dicotyledons (dicots). Monocots are so called because they germinate and sprout with a single 'cotyledon' or embryonic leaf, in their seed. Their leaves are typically slender, with parallel ribs, and sprout straight from the stem. The flowers have sepals and petals in whorls of three. Grasses (Gramineae) and orchids (Orchidaceae) are significant monocot families, both well represented in the Andes. Dicots have seedlings with two, rather than one, cotyledons. Their stems typically branch out and bear leaves with networks of veins. Their flowers are arranged in sets of four or five petals and sepals. There are many more dicotyledon families than monocotyledons, and they include the daisies (Compositae), cacti (Cactaceae), legumes (Leguminosae), roses (Rosaceae) and potatoes (Solanaceae). Monocots are often regarded as more primitive than dicots, as they appear simpler in design. However, botanists agree that monocots actually evolved from dicots, rather than the other way round.

Top Seeding pampas grass (*Cortaderia* sp.) (HP)
Above Andean Blueberry (*Berberis lutea*) (HP)

DICOTYLEDONS
Alders

Alder trees (genus *Alnus*) are common in areas of secondary growth in cloud forest habitats. However, in many areas, such as the upper region of the Manu road, they form unique stands of spectacular forests, with very tall trees (up to 25m) that are ghostly white in appearance and draped in mosses. These forests also form an important component of the larger Andean cloudforest ecosystem. Many of the most colourful and gregarious Andean bird species, such as the blue-banded toucanet (*Aulacorhynchus coeruleicinctus*) and white-collared jay (*Cyanolyca viridicyana*) can be found foraging in these woodlands, while others such as the spectacular chestnut-crested cotinga (*Ampelion stresemanni*) use the trees for their nesting habitat. First the Incas and then the Spanish used alder trunks for beams and lintels in buildings. Nowadays, the wood is still used to make doors, windows and even packing crates.

Alpines

Plant cover at altitudes of over 3,000m is sparse, consisting mostly of species that are adapted to the harsh conditions of intense solar heat during the day, biting frost by night and frequent snow. Alpines are the plants most typical of this habitat. They are typically small and low-lying, and have evolved to make the most of the

Alnus woodland (AW/FL)

Peruvian rock purslane (*Calandrinia umbellata*) is a tenacious species that grows low to the ground. (HP)

protection afforded by rock crevices, loose debris and other plant life. One species that specialises in growing in rock crevices is *Senecio tephrosiodes*. The leaves of this herbaceous plant are often combined with those of two other medicinal plants to treat coughs. Alpines belonging to the genus *Nototriche* have 'blanketing' or low-lying leaves to help them gather sunshine. These leaves are often used to make a tea to treat colic. Alpines such as *Stangea henrici* (also known as *Roseton* because of its resemblance to roses) that grow at elevations above 4,600m can also resist freezing, courtesy of 'antifreeze' chemicals in their sap.

Being so hardy and tenacious, alpine plants can survive on poor soils – often little more than grit and stones with a small quantity of humus. They also display vividly coloured flowers, which have evolved to attract as many pollinating insects as possible during the brief windows of opportunity that their habitat affords. Many of these fascinating plants are easily found on the trails and trekking routes of the Huascáran National Park, in the Cordillera Blanca of central Peru, or in the Pampas Galeras National Reserve. In fact most popular trekking routes in the Cusco area will reveal a selection of species.

Cacti

A number of plants in the Peruvian Andes have prickles and spines. This is to protect them against foraging herbivores, which would otherwise find them a tempting alternative to grasses and alpine herbs. The most familiar of these are surely the cacti. Cacti are adapted to survive in habitats that suffer regular droughts, hence they are sometimes known as known as 'xerophytic' (dry-loving) plants. They have evolved large spines to reduce evaporation and conserve water, and they can also store water by expanding considerably when the rains arrive.

The prickly pears of the genus *Opuntia* are among the most common cacti found in the Peruvian Andes. Their name comes from their large pear-shaped, prickly fruits that are often cultivated for human consumption. Known as tuna in Peru, these are a popular treat not to be missed at any local market when in season. Cacti such as *Opuntia flocossa* (known locally as *Warqu*) form colonies shaped like large cushions, over 60cm in diameter. Their flowers have bright red petals with yellow centres, and their yellow fruits eventually ripen to an orange colour. These species grow in the puna zone, above 3,800m, and are an important food source for several hummingbirds, including the endemic black-breasted hillstar (*Oreotrochilus melanogaster*) of central Peru.

Another interesting and distinctive group of cacti are those of the genus *Oreocereus*. These are commonly refered to as 'woolly' cacti or 'old men' cacti due to their coating of whitish hair-like fibres. Given that these cacti grow at high altitude, one might presume that their fleeces had evolved as insulation against the cold. However, insulation would

Peruvian old man cactus (*Oreocereus lanas*) (KZ/A)

make little or no difference to an organism that generates no heat. In fact, their purpose is to reduce moisture loss as far as possible by preventing air-flow around the bodies of the cacti. Two species commonly found in the Peruvian Andes are the old man of the Andes (*Oreocereus celsianus*) and the Peruvian old man (*Oreocereus lanas*). Both are equipped with antifreeze chemicals in their sap that make them frost resistant.

Some cacti grow to tree-like proportions. The candelabra cactus (*Isolatocereus dumortieri*) grows by branching out with vertical stems from a small base – as its common name suggests. It can exceed 10m in height and is usually found in desert habitats, where the soil is poor and sandy.

The sacred flower of the Incas (*Cantuta buxifolia*) (HP)

Cantutas

No account of the flora of the Peruvian Andes would be complete without mentioning the cantutas, in particular *Cantua buxifolia*, which is the national flower of Peru. Known locally as *Qantuta*, *Cantuta* or *Flor del Inca* ('flower of the Incas'), this plant is often found festooning hedgerows with its platform arrangement of bright flowers. The Incas dedicated it to their sun god, and used its pattern on their ceramics and textiles. The flowers vary in colour: purple, red, pink, white and yellow are the most common, though sometimes they are streaked in various colour combinations. They are tubular in shape, and open out in a trumpet-like fashion to hang pendulously. The plant itself stands above head height, with erect stems, arching branches and small fleshy leaves. Cantutas cannot tolerate the sub-zero temperatures of very high altitudes and are more commonly found growing in shrublands in the 2,500–3,200m zone. They are often grown as an ornamental plant in town plazas, such as in Cusco, and are a common sight in the Sacred Valley of the Incas. The world's largest hummingbird, the giant hummingbird (*Patagonia gigas*), often feeds on Cantuta nectar.

THE CONTROVERSIAL COCA

No book concerning Andean plants could fail to mention the coca bush (*Erythroxylon coca*) and leaf. Coca has been part of Andean life for millennia and is woven into the very fabric of Peruvian society. When chewed, it acts as a stimulant to help suppress hunger, thirst and fatigue, and fortifies the body against the effects of altitude. In Incan times it was so prized that only the nobility were allowed to use it, but after the arrival of the Spanish conquistadors it was introduced widely throughout Peru and has played an important part in life ever since. Men chew it whilst tilling fields and women use it to ease the pain of childbirth. It is easily purchased at any highland market and often an infusion known as mate de coca is offered to guests on arrival at mountain hotels, particularly in Cusco, to alleviate symptoms of altitude sickness. The leaves contain 14 alkaloids, one of which is the narcotic cocaine. Some of the nonpsychoactive chemicals are still used for the flavouring of the popular beverage Coca-Cola, but the narcotic cocaine was removed from the drink in 1903 due to public outcry. The cocaine trade is a nasty one – not only because of the drug abuse

Andean woman harvesting coca leaves (EP/A)

and gang violence, but also from the wide deforestation of Peruvian cloud forests, especially in the Huallaga river valley. The leaf in its original form, however, is perfectly legal and universally used in the Peruvian Andes. Many tourists try it when hiking the Inca trail.

Coffee family

The coffee family (Rubiaceae) is an important component part of the cloud forest flora and makes up the fourth largest plant family, after Asteraceae (daisies), Orchidaceae (orchids) and Leguminoseae (legumes). Coffee plants (*Coffea arabica* and *C. canephora*), however, are not native to Peru, having originated from Africa. The prefix 'Rubi' refers to the typically reddish or ruby-like berries borne by most species in this family. Inside these are two hemispherical seeds, which are usually edible. Most of the family are woody shrubs or trees, but a few are herbaceous.

There are five recognised species of cinchona tree (*Cinchona pubescens*). Otherwise known as the quinine tree, its bark once played a vital role in supplying the drug quinine. Known in the 18th century as 'Peruvian bark' or 'Jesuit's bark', it was used for treating malaria until synthetic drugs became available. Malaria was once the

Chinchona tree (*Chinchona pubescens*), also known as 'Jesuit's bark' (HA/NV)

scourge of the world, a disease so deadly it changed the course of history, devastating armies and laying waste to great civilisations. It was not until the discovery of the cinchona tree that it could be treated. Even so, up to three million people die of malaria each year, most of them in sub-Saharan Africa. The flowers of the palicoureas (genus *Palicourea*), small woody shrubs commonly found in cloud forests, are a good source of nectar for resident hummingbirds, while Psychotria species are traditionally used by local peoples in the preparation of herbal remedies for psychological ailments.

Compositae

This group of plants is more commonly known as the daisy or aster family, and is sometimes referred to as the Asteraceae. In the Peruvian Andes, it contains more species than any other family of flowering plants. This isn't surprising, as the family accounts for around 10% of the planet's flowers. The name 'Compositae' derives from the flowers' composite floral heads (known as 'capitula'), made from many individual blooms crammed so tightly together that they resemble a single flower. What most people refer to as the petals are actually modified leaves called bracts. This arrangement is the secret of the family's success, and assists in cross-pollination, thus promoting genetic variation. In addition it helps the flowers to stand out in the crowd of other plants, so that pollinating insects visit them more frequently. Not all species, however, have their blooms arranged in the traditional daisy pattern and a multitude of other forms have evolved. These include inflorescent stems with tiered flowers, platforms of flowers on tiered stalks, and spheres of flowers radiating from a central point.

The Compositae, like many abundant montane flower families of South America, are largely absent from lowland regions. This is because they are relict populations from a time when the landmasses of the northern hemisphere were conjoined into the super-continent Laurasia. It means that the mountainsides are, effectively, habitat 'islands' with the consequence that plants have evolved into species that are locally endemic to individual mountains or mountain chains.

A number of common Compositae species in the Peruvian Andes belong to the genus *Senecio*. These are commonly found in puna habitats at elevations above 4,000m. One species, *Senecio tephrosiodes*, is a tall, erect plant with bright yellow flowers that bloom in April. Andean communities typically use this species, known locally as *Wamanripa*, as a tea to treat coughs and, in central Peru, to flavour locally made rum. *Baccharis* is another important Andean genus of woody shrubs. Species such as *Baccharis genistelloides* (known locally as *Quima senqa*) have white flower heads but no normal leaves. Instead, each flower stem consists of three vertical 'wings' with indentations. This species grows in grasslands and montane forests at 3,500–4,500m. Water in which the plant has been boiled is used by many Andean communities to cure urinary tract infections.

Senecio canascens (HP)

Fuschias bring a splash of colour to the highlands. (HP)

Another common Compositae group found in the Peruvian Andes are the *Gynoxys* trees. These trees are typical of high-elevation habitats, above 3,300m. They are easily found along the highest treeline habitats of the Inca trail, and in the Abra Malaga region, above the town of Ollantaytambo in the Sacred Valley. *Tocacho* trees are a common source of firewood for remote, High Andean communities, and are often planted as hedges to demarcate boundaries between farms and houses.

Sauco tree

The *Sauco* tree (*Sambucus peruviana*) is another species typical of inter-Andean valleys, and is cultivated around many houses and gardens throughout Peru. This was formerly considered to be a member of the honeysuckle family (Caprifoliaceae), but recent research has shown that it actually belongs to the Adoxaceae family, which includes all the common elders. *Sauco* trees produce small and highly edible purplish-black fruits that are prepared both locally and commercially for jams and sweets. Their wood is often used for building materials and for making *quenas* – traditional Andean flutes.

Ericas

The Ericaceae plants are synonymous with the term 'ericaceous', which describes the acid soil in which they grow. Most species have very shallow roots, designed to penetrate layers of rotting vegetation or humus. As a result, they are prevalent in cloud forest habitats and can also be found in Andean marshland, bogs and heathlands. The laurel-like genus *Demosthenesia* contains a number of species endemic to the Cusco region, including *Demosthenesia cordifolia* and *Demosthenesia vilcabambensis*, both of which are considered endangered. The *Gaultheria* genus contains shrubs known as teaberries or wintergreens, which produce edible red berries from urn-shaped flowers. Another genus, *Vaccinium*, contains the blueberry, bilberry and cranberry. The Andean blueberry (*Vaccinium floribundum*) grows in the under-storey of cloud forest edges at 2,800–4,000m. Known locally as *Macha-macha* or *Congama*, this slender shrub, which may grow 2–3m tall, has pink flowers with deep green foliage, which give it a handsome appearance. Its small, round, highly prized fruit is sold in village markets throughout the Peruvian Andes.

Fuschias

The genus *Fuchsia* is part of the Onagraceae family, which also comprises evening primroses, purslanes and willow-herbs. The beauty of fuchsias caused a stir when they were first identified by Charles Plumier in the late 17th century, and they were named in 1753 in honour of the 16th-century German botanist Leonhart Fuchs. In fact, legend has it that a British sailor brought the first fuchsia back to Europe in the 1790s for his mother. There are about 100–110 species, the vast majority of which are native to Andean cloud forests. Fuchsias typically have pendulous, tubular flowers that open at the end to reveal their reproductive organs. The petals and sepals are often differently coloured to give a two-tone effect, in pinks, reds or mauves, depending on the species. Species found in the Peruvian Andes include *Fuchsia andrei* (all red), *Fuchsia apetala* (pink and white), *Fuchsia austromontana* (pink and yellow), *Fuchsia denticulata* (pink and greenish), *Fuchsia inflata* (penis-shaped, pink and green) and *Fuchsia simplicicaulis* (slender and red). The plants vary in form from small bushes to large shrubs. Some, such as *Fuchsia inflata*, are epiphytic and can be found in cloud forest regions growing in rock crevices or on tree branches.

Myrtles

Myrtle is the common name for the Myrtaceae, a mostly tropical family of woody shrubs and trees found especially in the Americas and Australia. Myrtles have evergreen leaves that contain aromatic, volatile oils, and many also have conspicuous and colourful flowers. The family is of considerable economic value throughout the world, yielding timber, resins, oils, spices and edible fruits. Andean bog myrtle (*Myrteola nummularia*) is commonly found on the raised portions of high Andean bogs, usually around blankets of sphagnum mosses (*Sphagnum magellanicum*). This slow-growing, stocky plant has evolved to tolerate the high levels of ultraviolet radiation in the High Andes. Its very short leaves are often used to make teas, and its aromatic fruit is considered a regional delicacy, raw or cooked. It produces a carpet of low branches that can take root, enabling it to propagate without relying solely on seed dispersal.

THE UBIQUITOUS EUCALYPTUS

Botany Bay near modern-day Sydney was named for the rich source of new species discovered by Sir Joseph Banks, the botanist on the famous Cook expedition of 1770. Many have subsequently been introduced around the world, and eucalyptus plantations have been a part of the Andean landscape in Peru since the early 20th century. The species predominantly planted is *Eucalyptus globules* (also known as Tasmanian blue gum. See picture on page 32.), which was first planted in Ecuador and quickly spread from there. Local communities soon realised its value and contributed to its propagation. It grows very quickly relative to native Andean trees, and it grows straight, which makes it a useful plant for firewood and roofing beams. In the Peruvian Andes it has largely replaced forests of the slow-growing native *Polylepis* trees, whose numbers have been greatly depleted over the centuries by local people in search of timber and firewood. Today Eucalyptus trees are a valuable commodity for trade between Andean communities and other parts of the country. Their presence in the Peruvian Andes is less welcome to conservation biologists, since the trees prevent the natural establishment and progression of endemic plants. However, they do provide a valuable source of nectar for a number of hummingbird species, most noticeably the endangered purple-backed sunbeam (*Aglaeactis aliciae*), which is endemic to the La Libertad region of north Peru.

Nasturtiums and legumes

The name 'nasturtium' is thought to derive from the Latin for 'nose-twister' or 'nose-tormentor' in reference to the pungent, hot flavour of the leaves and flowers, which are used in salads. The common nasturtium plant of the Andes, *Tropaeolum majus*, is often referred to as Indian cress, because it has a similar taste to Old World watercress. The two species are indeed related, both being members of the family *Tropaeolaceae*. Indian cress is naturally a climbing vine, typical of cloud forest habitats, particularly where the forests have been disturbed. However, non-climbing forms

Lupin bush (HP)

Eucalyptus tree (RW)

have been bred for cultivation. In the Peruvian Andes, the montane nasturtium *Tropaeolum polyphyllum* forms large grey-green mats over boulder scree on mountain slopes, with shocks of yellow-orange flowers wreathing the end of each stem. *Tropaeolum* species are readily identified by the horn-like spur protruding from the rear of each flower.

The word 'legume' is derived from the French *légume*, which refers to any kind of vegetable. It has two closely related meanings: first, the common name for a plant species belonging to the family Leguminosae; second, a type of fruit that is characteristic of leguminous plants. Leguminosae is one of the most important Neotropical tree families. It is the predominant family of slender vines, and some lianas and herbs. A very familiar group of leguminous plants found in the Andes are the lupins (genus *Lupinus*), which are cultivated as garden flowers all over the world. The spectacular giant *Lupinus weberbauerii* and the smaller *Lupinus mutabillis* (known locally as *tarwi*, meaning multi-coloured) are 1–1.5m-tall herbaceous plants, with lavender pea-like flowers. They are found at 4,200–4,600m near the natural treeline throughout the mountains of Peru. The leaves of many lupins are described as 'digitate' because they resemble spread hands. The seeds, like those of most legumes, are borne in pods. These split open with an energetic twist when ripe, scattering the seeds some distance from the parent plant. Another common montane legume is the Andean milkvetch (*Astragalus garbancillo*). Known locally as *Jusqa*, it grows to about 1m in height in overgrazed pasturelands, and is readily identified by its white flowers and compound feathery leaves.

The *Pisonay* tree is one of the tallest legumes of the Peruvian Andes. This tall, distinctive species belongs to the genus *Erythrina*, and is native to the lower foothills and cloud forest habitats below 2,000m. *Pisonay* trees were first cultivated by the Incas, who regarded the species as sacred. Now they can often be found decorating the plazas of Andean towns. Species such as *Erythrina edulis* are easily recognisable by their numerous, dense clusters of brilliant scarlet-red tubular flowers that are pollinated by many hummingbirds.

One of the most common legumes of Peru's inter-Andean valleys is the *Retama* (*Spartium junecum*), commonly known as Spanish broom. This perennial, evergreen shrub is most often found along roadsides, rail tracks, city plazas and gardens, where it can exceed 1m in height. It is easily recognisable by its clusters of long, bright yellow, pea-shaped flowers that bloom at the end of long stems.

TARWI: THE NEXT SOYBEAN?

Tarwi (pronounced *tar-wee*), the seeds of the lupin bush, contain more than 40% protein – at least as much as cultivated protein crops such as peas, beans, soybeans and peanuts. In addition, the seeds contain almost 20% oil, as much as soybeans and several other oilseed crops. *Tarwi* would thus appear to be a ready source of protein for food and feed, as well as a good source of vegetable oil for cooking, margarine and other processed food products. This beautiful crop could also qualify as an ornamental: its brilliant blue blossoms bespangle the upland fields of the Indians of Peru, Bolivia and Ecuador. In Cusco, the former Inca capital, baskets of the usually bone-white *tarwi* seeds are a customary sight in the markets. These are most often served in soups and are outstandingly nutritious. The protein they contain is rich in lysine, the vital amino acid. Mixing *tarwi* and cereals makes a food that, in its balance of amino acids, is almost ideal for humans. With these exceptional nutritional qualities, *tarwi* might become another 'soybean' in importance, but it is not yet cultivated on a wider scale.

Pepper trees

Pepper trees (Annonaceae) are fairly typical of the dry inter-Andean habitats of Peru. Species such as *Schinus molle*, known locally as *Molle* in southern Peru, can grow 5–6m tall. This species is a common sight in the arid scrub around the little-known Inca ruins and lakes at Huacarpay, only 30 minutes from Cusco. It is a beautiful plant, with a number of local and commercial uses. The Incas once used the resin to embalm mummies. Today, however, the wood is used for building material, while the ashes are used for making a particular tanning agent and also to make soap. *Molle* trees have tightly packed clusters of small, globular, reddish fruits that hang vertically from the outermost branches and are a food source for many Andean birds. The fruit is also used in the manufacture of local honey, vinegar and a variety of other condiments. Oils extracted from the plant's leaves are used commercially in the manufacture of both perfumes and toothpaste.

Molle trees have been used for everything from embalming mummies to making soap. (RW)

Potatoes and allies

Perhaps the most famous plant to originate from the Peruvian Andes, and certainly the most important commercially, is the potato (*Solanum tuberosum*), now a staple food for millions in temperate regions around the world. The potato is a member of the nightshade family (*Solanaceae*), which is well represented throughout South America. There is considerable debate about how it first made its way to Europe. Some authorities claim that Sir Walter Raleigh was responsible for introducing it in 1596, although Sir Walter's travels never took him to a region in which he would have encountered the plant. Some German authorities claim that the licensed British pirate Sir Francis Drake was responsible in 1579, having made landfall at Colombia. However, it is now apparent that the Spanish had already brought it back to Europe by 1570. The conquistador Don Juan Castellanos certainly made the first written account of the potato in 1537 as part of a military report on raiding an Inca village in Peru during a search for gold and silver.

As well as cooking and eating potatoes, Incas also made raw flour from dehydrated potatoes called *chuño*, which they added to other dishes. There are still many types of potato cultivated in the Andes, and also many wild species, including *Solanum andigenum* and *Solanum juzepczuki*. The wide genetic variety provides today's Andean people with potatoes of different textures and flavours, which is important at altitudes where other crops will not grow easily. Some strains are frost resistant and the tubers always store well naturally below ground. The wide variety also means Peruvian potatoes have a wealth of resistance to diseases. Elsewhere in the world, by contrast, potato farmers who have concentrated on growing single varieties have often lost their livelihood to fungal diseases, such as potato blight (*Phytophthora infestans*), or pests, such as the Colorado beetle (*Leptinotarsa decemlineata*). In the Peruvian Andes, Andean potato weevils (*Premnotrypes* spp.) are a specific problem because their large white larvae infest and destroy plants by boring their way into the tubers.

FIRST FREEZE-DRIED FOOD

The ancient Peruvians were the inventors of the freeze-dry process. The environment was perfect during the winter dry season in the Andes, when frosty nights and sub-zero temperatures alternated with hot, sunny dry days. The production of these freeze-dried potatoes, known as *chuño*, takes about five days. After harvest, the potatoes are selected – typically small ones for ease of processing. They are spread closely on flat ground and allowed to freeze with low night temperatures for approximately three nights. By day they are exposed to the sun and trampled by foot. This eliminates what little water is still retained by the potatoes, and removes their skins, enabling subsequent freezing. They are then exposed to the cold for two more nights. Two basic varieties are then obtained: *moraya*, by 'washing' the frozen potatoes in river pools then allowing them to dry in the sun; *chuño*, from simply freezing, trampling and refreezing, after which it is simply sun-dried. The resulting products can be stored for a long time, even years, and can be made into flour or rehydrated in soups. On one mountain pass in Peru there are piles of ancient freeze-dried potatoes, left by a retreating Inca army fleeing the Spanish invaders.

An inedible member of the potato family is the angel's trumpet (*Datura arborea*), which is a tree that bears large, white, funnel-shaped flowers. It is highly toxic, like many members of the solanaceous group, being packed full of narcotic alkaloids. Apparently small doses of its pollen make an effective cure for insomnia, although one might be forgiven for thinking that the fear of being poisoned would have the exact opposite effect! Inca priests once used a *Datura* preparation to induce their paroxysms – sudden attacks of emotional expression – that they attributed to their communications with the gods. This was undoubtedly a powerful tool in maintaining the Inca empire. Other members of this genus include the shrubs *Datura chlorantha*, *Datura sanguina* and *Datura cornigera*, which have yellowish, orangey and whitish flowers respectively. These are used by *curanderos*, or healers, in their attempts to travel into the spirit world.

Top Flowering potato plant (HP)
Above Some varieties of Peruvian potato (HP)

Another noteworthy genus in the nightshade family is *Nicotiana*, which includes the Virginian tobacco plant (*Nicotiana tabacum*). The genus is named in honour of the French diplomat and scholar Juan Nicot, who first introduced tobacco to France in around 1560. *Nicotiana* plants are more commonly found in the inter-Andean valleys of Peru. One species to note is *Nicotiana glauca*, a small woody shrub whose large bunches of yellow flowers are a favourite food source for many Andean hummingbirds.

In central Peru, the leaves of *Nicotiana thyrsiflora* (known locally as *Tutuma*) are heated and rubbed over joints to alleviate rheumatism.

Proteas

Proteas in Latin America are quintessentially Andean, though many other plants in the same family are found in southern Africa and Australia. In the Peruvian Andes they occur on the more windswept ridge tops, and at the edge of high-elevation cloud and elfin forest habitats. Species such as *Oreocalis grandiflora*, known in southern Peru as *Chacpa*, are easily recognised by their slender appearance and spectacular spike-like arrangement of pink flowers that can grow up to 5–6m tall. These flowers are an important food source for the various hummingbird species, such as the diminutive scaled metaltail (*Metallura aeneocauda*), that are restricted to

Andean raspberry (*Rubus glaucus*) (FNS)

this narrow, timberline zone. Andean people harvest *Chacpa* trees for their slender and highly flexible branches, which they use to make baskets. The leaves are often chewed as a preventative measure against tooth decay.

Rose family

The family Rosaceae gets its name from *Rosa*, the genus for roses, which are plants of the northern hemisphere. Most woody members of this family are restricted to Andean habitats in Peru. Species of Rosaceae herbs, belonging to the genus *Rubus*, are typically arching canes or clambering vines, and are often found in disturbed cloud forest habitats (they can also be seen alongside roads that bisect the humid eastern slopes, such as the roads to the Manu National Park in southern Peru). The Andean raspberry (*Rubus glaucus*), known locally as *Shirapoco*, belongs to the same genus as the familiar raspberry (*Rubus idaeus*) and blackberry (*Rubus fruticosus*). It bears 25mm-long, edible fruits that vary in colour from red to black. The plant is often used as living fencing to corral livestock.

Another popular member of this family is the *Capuli* tree (*Prunus capuli*), which was introduced into Peru from Central America by the Spanish. This species sometimes grows up to 8m tall, and its edible red or black berries are harvested in January–March, either to make jam or to be dried for use in liqueurs. Its leaves are a natural source of amygdalin, which has both sedative and cardiovascular properties.

POLYLEPIS: PERU'S MOST THREATENED FOREST

Polylepis forest occurs above cloud level at 3,500–5,000m. It exists as islands of woody vegetation, surrounded by paramo or puna grasslands and shrub communities, and comprises mainly evergreen trees of the genus *Polylepis* (Rosaceae), which are highly drought tolerant. Known locally as *Queuña*, the largest *Polylepis* trees can grow to 18m in height, with trunks 2m across. The trunk and branches are laminated with brown-reddish bark that peels off in paper-like sheets, and often have mosses and lichens growing on them. The remaining areas of *Polylepis* woodland are the relics of a once-widespread habitat, reduced by chronic overgrazing and burning to scattered fragments. *Polylepis* woodlands continue to be cleared throughout their Andean range, and some areas of Peru (for example, the Mantaro Valley, near Junín, in central Peru) have been completely deforested. The total *Polylepis* forest cover in Peru is now estimated at 700–1500km², no more than 2–3% of its former range.

A number of specialised bird species are restricted to these forests. As a consequence of the catastrophic habitat loss, many are now among the most threatened birds in Latin America. Species such as the royal cinclodes (*Cinclodes aricomae*), ash-breasted tit-tyrant (*Anairetes alpinus*) and white-browed tit-spinetail (*Leptasthenura xenothorax*) have extremely small populations in the few patches that remain – the entire global population of royal cinclodes is thought to number fewer than 200 individuals. In the Cordillera Vilcanota, these forests and their endangered bird species are now the focus of a major conservation and habitat restoration programme, organised by the Peruvian non-governmental organisation Asociación Ecosistemas Andinos (ECOAN), which is working in partnership with the many indigenous Andean communities. Two of the best areas to see these endangered *Polylepis* forests are located in the Sacred Valley, near Cusco; the Mantanay Valley, situated above the town of Yanahuara; and the forests of Yanacocha, situated above the village of Huaocari.

The layered bark of the Polylepis, or Queuña tree, is highly distinctive. (TM/SAP)

Saxifrages

Escallonia trees belong to the saxifrage family. Known locally as *chachacomo* trees, they are among the most ecologically important genera of the cloud and elfin forests. Species such as *Escallonia resinosa* are often the dominant tree in these humid, high-altitude forests. *Chachacomo* trees can reach approximately 6m tall (although the smaller *Escallonia* woody shrubs grow to about 3m). They produce high-quality wood for building, and their leaves are often used to produce reddish and purple dyes. These trees are highly resistant to drought, and are planted throughout the Peruvian Andes to stabilise mountain terraces and help prevent erosion. Some spectacular *chachacomo* trees can be easily be found along the fairly short half-day hike to Lago Yanacocha, above the village of Huaocari in the Sacred Valley.

MONOCOTYLEDONS
Agaves

Agaves are very similar to the bromeliads in form. They are succulent plants that grow only in dry inter-Andean valleys, particularly around the Cusco region. The word 'agave' is derived from *agauos*, the Ancient Greek word for 'illustrious'. The two species most familiar in the Peruvian Andes are *Agave americana*, also known as American aloe, and *Furcrea andina*. Both are known locally as *Maguey* in southern Peru. The former is bluish and the latter green.

Agaves were very useful plants for the Incas, who used their leaf fibres to make ropes and knit suspension bridges and sandals. Soaps can also be produced from the plant. Its stiff leaves are edged with protective serrations and terminal spines, while

Fibres from the American aloe were put to good use by the Incas. (RW)

the upright, flat-topped flowers are typically arranged in a tiered fashion on an erect stem. Each plant flowers only once and then dies, having exhausted itself of nutrients in the process of reproduction. Another name for *Agave americana* is the century plant, because of a belief that it flowers only once every 100 years. In fact, flowering happens only when conditions are appropriate, which may be at any time from five years of age to several decades.

Amaranths

The amaranths (Amaranthaceae), collectively known as pigweed, are a widespread and cosmopolitan family of tropical plants. They have dense green or reddish clusters of tiny flowers and include several weeds, ornamentals and food plants. The best-known species in the Peruvian Andes are kiwicha and quinua. Local people have cultivated kiwicha for more than 4,000 years, although after the Inca empire it was almost forgotten. Nowadays kiwicha has been rediscovered as a valuable source of nutrition, with its grains providing important vitamins such as calcium, phosphorus, iron, potassium and zinc. It is used in soups, salads and stews as a source of energy. The grains can also be toasted and used as a cereal, and the flour used in baking – either alone or combined with other ingredients, such as wheat flour. Quinua was held to be sacred by the Incas, who knew it as *chisaya mama* or 'mother of all grains', and the Inca emperor would use gold implements to sow the first seeds of the season. During the Spanish conquest, quinoa was scorned by the Spanish colonists as 'food for Indians', and even actively suppressed, due to its status in indigenous, non-Christian ceremonies.

LOST FOOD OF THE INCAS

Quinoa and kiwicha were of great nutritional importance within pre-Columbian Andean civilisations, being secondary only to the potato. In contemporary times these crops have become highly appreciated for their nutritional value, and the United Nations has classified them as a supercrop for their very high protein content (12–18%). Unlike wheat or rice, which are low in lysine, quinoa and kiwicha contain a balanced set of essential amino acids for humans, making them an unusually complete foodstuff. This means it takes less quinoa or kiwicha protein to meet one's

Andean girls gathering Quinua (HP)

needs than wheat protein. They are also a good source of dietary fibre and, being gluten-free, are easy to digest. This combination of characteristics has earned quinoa consideration as a possible crop in NASA's controlled ecological life-support system for long-duration manned spaceflights.

Puya Raimondii has the largest flower spike of any plant in the world. (HP)

Bromeliads

The name 'bromeliad' has been attributed to French explorer-priest Charles Plumier, who chose the name in honour of the 18th-century Swedish botanist Olaf Bromel for a plant he encountered while exploring the Caribbean region. Most bromeliads are restricted to lowland rainforest, but a few genera make their home in the High Andes. Other species, particularly of the genus *Guzmania*, are common components of Peruvian cloud forest habitats. Bromeliads are relatively simple plants. Typical species such as *Tillandsia* have rosettes of tapering, fleshy leaves that funnel and collect water at their base. This water often provides a microhabitat for invertebrates, and sometimes even small frogs. Bromeliads bear their flowers on spikes that grow from the central point between the leaves. The impressive rock walls surrounding Machu Picchu are covered with thousands of *Tillandsia* bromeliads.

GIANT FLOWER OF THE ANDES

Puya raimondii is the world's largest bromeliad species. The name 'puya' was derived from the Mapuche Indian (Chilean) word meaning 'point'. It refers to the

spectacular flower-spike, which contains over 8,000 whitish-green blooms that turn purplish in colour with age. The puya flowers relatively infrequently. However, when it does, the flower-spike reaches around 10m in height. This, the tallest flower-spike in the world, protrudes high above the dense basal cluster of thick, bayonet-like leaves, which are edged with defensive spines as protection from browsing animals. The flowers can attract dozens of hummingbirds of several species, which congregate to exploit this brief nectar bonanza. The puya can also withstand the considerable changes from day- to night-time temperatures thanks to a chemical in its sap that acts as antifreeze. One of the most accessible and best places to see the *Puya raimondii* 'forests' is along the road that passes from Pachacoto (near Huaraz) to Huallanca, through the Cordillera Blanca and the Parque Nacional Huascaran in central Peru.

The tightly packed flowers of *Puya raimondii* (HP)

Guanacos grazing on *ichu* grassland (HP)

Grasses and sedges

The dominant plants of many high Andean habitats are grasses, of which there are many species. These are flowering plants, with jointed stems, narrow leaves and spikes of diminutive flowers that rely on the wind for pollination. Tuft-forming grasses are also an essential component of bogs and marshlands. Some species of grasses and sedges, such as *zea* (maize or Indian corn), are grown by Peruvians for food and other uses. The flowers of grasses are atypical among flowering plants as they lack petals and sepals. This is because they are not designed to attract insects for pollination. Instead, they produce a large quantity of dusty pollen, so that individual plants are cross-pollinated when the wind blows. Dominant genera of puna and altiplano grasslands of southern and central Peru, and paramo grasslands in northern and central Peru, include fescues (*Festuca*), bush grasses (*Calamagrostis*), bent grasses (*Agrostis*), bromes (*Bromus*), grey rushes (*Juncus*) and

Totora reeds on Lake Junín. (HP)

feather grasses (*Stipa*). The common native needle grass is known as *Stipa ichu*, though *ichu* is the universal name for all bunch grass. This grass is the traditional thatch used for roofing in isolated highland villages. Today it is also the main source of food for grazing alpacas and llamas, though overgrazing is a problem in many areas. Many native grasses can be seen around the Acjanacu guard station, at the southern tip of Manu National Park, above the town of Paucartambo.

Bamboos are woody evergreen plants belonging to the true grass family, Poaceae. Some species are giants, and constitute the largest members of the grass family. The most common genus in the Andes is *Chusquea*, which comprises arching, slender montane bamboo species that form dense thickets in cloud and elfin forest habitats above 2,000m. Extensive tracts of *Chusquea* bamboo can be found along the road to Manu National Park in southern Peru, and high in the Carpish Mountains, near Huanuco, in central Peru. Many endemic Peruvian bird species, including Parodi's hemispingus (*Hemispingus parodi*) and rufous-browed hemispingus (*Hemispingus rufosuperciliaris*), are restricted to these bamboo habitats.

The Floating Islands (*Islas Flotantes*) of the indigenous Uros community are among the most popular tourist destinations in the southern Andean region of Puno. The lives of the Uros people are dependent on the *totora* reeds (*Juncus andicola*) that grow in the shallow waters around Lake Titicaca. These reeds are actually used to construct the floating islands, which now support several buildings, a school, restaurants and souvenir shops. The Uros also use these reeds to make boats and numerous handicrafts. In Lake Junín, central Peru, *totora* reeds are the essential habitat for the endemic Junín rail (*Laterallus tuerosi*). This is one of Peru's most secretive and endangered bird species, and very few ornithologists have ever seen one.

SACRED BEER OF THE INCAS

Chicha is the working man's favourite beverage in the rural Andes. During the Inca empire women were taught the techniques of brewing *chicha* in *Acllahuasis* (womens' schools). The drink is traditionally prepared from a specific kind of yellow maize, called *jora*, and is usually referred to as *chicha de jora*. It has a pale straw colour, a slightly milky appearance and a slightly sour aftertaste that is reminiscent of hard apple cider. *Chicha* is drunk either young and sweet or mature and strong, and contains only 1–3% alcohol. This drink came to play a critical role in the economics of the empire. It was called *aqa* in Quechua, the language of the High Andes, and *kusa* in Aymara, the language of the altiplano and low country. But the Spaniards named it *chicha*, a word they derived from the Spanish *chichal*, meaning 'saliva' or 'to spit'. This name reflects the beer's early method of production, since Andean people had for centuries found saliva to be an effective means for converting starches in grains to fermentable sugars. Today sugar is used to start the fermentation process. It is a custom in rural Peru to hang red flowers (or nowadays a red plastic bag) on the end of a stick to proclaim that *chicha* is on sale – just like a pub sign in the UK.

Inca orchid (*Epidendrum* sp.) (HP)

Orchids

Many botanists have a particular passion for orchids and go out of their way to find them. The name 'orchid' is derived from that of a northern hemisphere genus, *Orchis*, which, in turn, comes from the Greek word *orkhis*, meaning testicle – in reference to the shape of the plants' tubers. This has given rise to the erroneous belief, in some parts of the world, that orchids possess aphrodisiac qualities. The roots of the plants are often fleshy or tuber-like and the flowers range widely in shape, size and colour. Each flower consists of three petals alternating with three sepals (the small leaf-like structures joined to the flowers). It is the shape of these sepals (sometimes called the lip, or labellum) that gives many species their own distinctive appearance. For instance, the lip of bee orchids (*Ophrys* spp.) is shaped like a bee, while those of epiphytic snail orchids (*Cochlioda* spp.), which grow on tree branches in cloud forest habitats, have curled crests that resemble snail shells.

The interior of orchid flowers is unusual among flowering plants. The male and female reproductive parts, known as stamens and stigmas respectively, are not separate, but fused in a central column-like structure, with the stamens above. Pollination is usually effected by nectar-feeding insects, especially bees, although some South American species are serviced by hummingbirds. Orchid pollen grains are also unusual because they form large pollen masses, called pollinia. These have a sticky section that attaches itself to hairs on pollinating insects, or feathers on hummingbirds. These winged pollinators then unwittingly fertilise the next flower they enter, by sticking the pollinia to the stigma. In the case of insect-pollinated orchids, the flowers are often designed to offer the bee different entrance and exit points. This is described as a 'cake-walk', since the insect inevitably becomes 'caked' in new pollen from the stamens and in turn 'cakes' the stigma with its pollen load on the way through.

Orchids manufacture prodigious quantities of seed, sometimes several million per plant, which are so small that they are carried on air currents to new locations. While this is a useful strategy for dispersal, each seed is completely devoid of food reserves – a weight-saving adaptation – and thus cannot germinate by its own volition. Most perish, but a few settle in a suitable place for germination. Every orchid species has a symbiotic (mutually beneficial) relationship with a particular fungus species, and the two must meet in order for each to begin its development. The mycelium of the fungus (the vegetative portion below ground) provides the nutrition and minerals that the orchid seeds require in order to germinate. Once established, the orchid then reciprocates by providing the fungus with nutrients from its roots. This 'mycorrhizal association' enables both the fungi and orchid to flourish in places where they would otherwise find it difficult to survive, such as in poor or thin soil, in rock crevices or on the bark of trees.

Most orchids can photosynthesise food from sunlight once they have leaves, but one group, known as saprophytes (for example, members of the genera *Wullschlaegelia* and *Uleiorchis*), have no chlorophyll and are often leafless. Their name is derived from the Greek word *sapros*, meaning rotten, and these species extract nutrients from the dead remains of other organisms. Orchids that grow on trees are described as epiphytes. They are not parasites, but merely use the trees as platforms on which to grow and find food. Some orchids, such as those belonging to the genera *Lycaste* and *Acineta*, grow at elevations where both soil and trees are in short supply, so they make do with crevices in rocks or shelves on cliff faces. These are known as lithophytes, or 'stone-plants'.

Over 70 genera of orchid are to be found in the Peruvian High Andes, further divided into hundreds of species. One of the best places to find them is in the cloud forest habitats around Machu Picchu. A common but very beautiful species is the Inca orchid (*Sobralia dichotoma*), which embellishes the Inca Trail leading to the ruins. Two species of *Masdevallia* orchid, *Masdevallia amabilis* and *Masdevallia veitchiana*, are stunning flowers, and highly regarded by local people who know them as *wakanki* or 'you will cry' flowers in appreciation of their sheer visual impact. Another species, *Epidendrum secundum*, has the charming local name *winay wayna*, meaning 'forever young'. This terrestrial species, with woody stems, leathery leaves, and yellow petals with purple or red spots inside, grows in large colonies – particularly around boulders. Other orchids found in the cloud forests, along the road from the ruins down to the town of Aguas Calientes, include the bat's face orchid (*Prosthechea vespa*) and dragon's face orchid (*Prosthechea fusca*).

Top Winay wayna orchid (*Epidendrum secundum*) (JB)

Right (*Masdevallia veitchiana*) orchid (AB)

MACHU PICCHU: ORCHID PARADISE

Machu Picchu is world renowned for its diversity of orchid species. We know that pre-Columbian indigenous groups knew and revered orchids, and there is some evidence that the Incas may have planted them as ornamental flowers along roads. The first modern reference to orchids at Machu Picchu was by the scientific discoverer Hiram Bingham, when in 1911 he described the lost city as being covered with 'vegetation and abundant orchids'. One book *A Synopsis of the Flora of Cusco* (F. Herrera, Lima, 1941) reported 55 species. In 1969 Dr Cesar Vargas Calderon catalogued 30 genera and 90 species in his publication *Ornamental Flora of Machu Picchu* (Universidad Nacional del Cusco, 1969). The recent publication, *Machu Picchu Orchids* (Eric Christenson, PROFONAMPE, 2003), cited more than 250 species in 75 genera within the Machu Picchu Historical Sanctuary. This is still thought to represent only half of the total number.

OTHER PLANTS
GYMNOSPERMS

The term 'gymnosperm' translates as 'naked seed', because these plants have seeds that are only partially protected during their development. The gymnosperms are a mixed bunch, thrown together by taxonomists only because they are not related to the plant groups that are placed above and below them in traditional taxonomic classification. The most familiar gymnosperms are conifer trees, but other families include cycads (Cycadaseae), gnetales (Gnetaceae) and podocarps (Podocarpaceae). The gnetale family includes evergreen shrubs of the genus *Ephedra* that have scale-like leaves on thin stems. These plants are the source of the drug ephedrine, which is a crystalline alkaloid used in treating asthma and hay fever. It constricts the blood vessels and widens the bronchial passages, countering the ailments' effects. In the Peruvian Andes, species such as American ephedra (*Ephedra americana*) can be found growing on rocky soils with various mosses at elevations over 4,500m. This species, known locally as *Pinco-pinco*, is the only gymnosperm found within Huascaran National Park, in central Peru. It is easily recognised by its white flowers and bright red berries that are produced on small, segmented tubular stems.

Peru's only native conifer is *Podocarpus glomeratus*, locally known as *Intimpa*, and this tree also occurs in the Peruvian Andes. The name 'podocarp' translates as 'foot-fruit', and is named after the toe-like extensions where the seeds protrude from the flesh of the olive-like fruits. The best-known site for *Podocarpus* in Peru is the Ampay National Sanctuary, an isolated area of montane forest near Abancay, only 4–5 hours' drive from Cusco. The trees grow as tall as 15m and can reach 3m in diameter. Due to the excellent quality of their wood, they were traditionally used for many things, including doors, furniture, beams and agricultural tools, while the branches were used to make corrals for animals. In recent times branches were also used as Christmas trees by the residents of Abancay, though this practice became obsolete with the advent of synthetic Christmas trees.

Running ground pine belongs to the club-moss group of ferns. (HP)

FERNS

In the Peruvian Andes the fern family (Pteridophyta) is represented by a dozen or more genera, comprising over 20 species. Ferns are primitive, flowerless plants that come in a variety of shapes and sizes, from small and moss-like to large and tree-like, though most are typically fern-like! All species share two diagnostic characteristics. First, the adult plants produce spores rather than seeds. These spores are very small, making them easy to disperse on air currents. When they germinate, they grow initially into miniature plants (called prothalli), which then develop the reproductive organs necessary to generate the mature ferns. Second, fern leaves contain water-conducting cells. This means ferns are not reliant on condensation for an external water supply, and can grow by tapping the ground for water with their roots. Fern species are notoriously difficult to identify, especially those from a common genus. Running ground pine (*Lycopodium clavatum*) is a

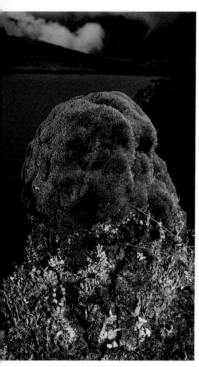

Sphagnum moss (HP)

montane species belonging to a group of ferns called club mosses, as they comprise moss-like branches that creep over the ground. Another species, *Lycopodium crassum*, is commonly found at 4,000–4,500m in Huascaran National Park, central Peru. Its shape has given it the local name of *Jacapa pishqun*, which means 'guinea-pig penis', and it is sometimes hung in the corner of guinea-pig pens to encourage them to breed.

MOSSES AND LIVERWORTS

Mosses are small, soft-bodied plants only 1–10cm tall. They typically grow close together in clumps or mats in damp and often shady conditions, as they need moisture for their reproduction and metabolism. Mosses do not have flowers or seeds, and their simple leaves often cover most of their thin wiry stems. Without roots to anchor themselves in the soil, they use tiny threads called rhizoids. The species that frequent montane habitats can cope with drought by drying out until rainfall arrives to spring them back into life. Mosses dominate Andean bog habitats, particularly members of the genus *Sphagnum*, which thrive in the acid conditions produced by decaying vegetation.

Liverworts get their name from their shape, certain species resembling the human liver. They are typically small plants that are often overlooked in the Peruvian Andes, and appear very much like flattened mosses. Liverworts can cover large areas of the ground, but may also grow on rocks, trees or any other suitable substrate. Like mosses, they prefer damp, shady locations. They are readily distinguished from mosses by their unicellular (single-celled) rhizoids; in mosses these are multicellular.

CHRISTMAS DECORATIONS

In households all across Peru at Christmas time, various mosses are used to decorate the traditional ceramic nativity scene, at little cost for people with no budget for pricier adornments. At the traditional Christmas Eve market in Cusco – called *Santuranticuy*, which means 'saints for sale' – image carvers and artisans sell a wide variety of figurines to liven up Christmas and fit out the nativity scenes that are set up in homes and parish churches. *Campesinos* (peasant farmers) come from miles around from the high puna to sell these mosses and other local plant species, either live or dried, to town and city dwellers.

FUNGI AND LICHENS

The best places to find fungi are in the many different forest habitats along the humid eastern slope of the Peruvian Andes. Identification of fungi here is very much in its infancy. However, walking trails through the cloud forest habitats of Abra Patricia in northern Peru, or in Manu National Park in southern Peru, will reveal a remarkable diversity of species. Many may eventually prove to be new to science.

The humid cloud forests are richly endowed with fungi. (HP)

Fungi are the major decomposers in all Andean ecosystems and play a critical role in many food webs. They were once classified as plants, but now we know that they are in fact more closely related to animals. Fungi fall into a number of different groups or 'divisions' including the Chytrids, the Zygomycetes, the Phycomycetes (or lower fungi), the Ascomycetes (or intermediate fungi) and the Basidiomycetes (or higher fungi). The last of these groups contains most of the familiar forms known as mushrooms. In fact, the structures that most people describe as toadstools, mushrooms or bracket fungi are actually only the fruiting bodies of the organisms, which they use to produce and disperse spores. The living and growing part is known as the mycelium and is usually hidden from view. It is a network of threads, called hyphae, that infests the material in which the fungus grows, such as decomposing leaf mould or rotting wood. Although invisible, the mycelia are often very extensive and form symbiotic associations with the roots of green plants, so that both organisms benefit by trading nutrients and minerals. Tulasnelloid fungi (a type of *chanterelle* fungus, belonging to the intermediate fungi group), for example, grow on various trees, and are an important symbiotic partner for arboreal orchids in cloud forest habitats.

Many species of fungi are also notorious pathogens. One species of Chytrid fungi,

Blue-dye lichen (HP)

Batrachochytrium dendrobatidis, is associated with global declines in many amphibian populations. The fungus kills frogs within 10 to 18 days of exposure, and although it is not known exactly how, experts suspect that the fungus causes severe respiratory problems by affecting the frogs' skin. Alarmingly, it has recently been found in the populations of two High Andean frog species, the marbled water-frog (*Telmatobius marmoratus*) and the puna frog (*Pleurodema marmorata*), both from Laguna Sibinacocha in the Cordillera Vilcanota.

Lichens can often be found growing on rocks in exposed boulder fields at elevations of over 4,000m in the Peruvian Andes. Such boulder fields are a common sight along the many trails through the valleys of Laras, Cancha-Cancha, Mantanay and Huilloc, in the Cordillera Vilcanota. Lichens are known as 'composite plants' because they comprise symbiotic partnerships between species of Ascomycete fungi and green algae (Cyanobacteria). This partnership means that lichens can obtain their water, minerals and nutrients from the atmosphere alone, enabling them to flourish in places where no other plants could survive.

MAMMALS

Puma (HP)

The class Mammalia contains the most advanced members of the animal kingdom. Mammals are characterised by a unique combination of features: they produce milk from mammary glands or specialised skin glands; they grow fur or hair; they possess three specialised and minute bones in the ear; and – like birds – they are endothermic, or warm-blooded. Taxonomists recognise two sub-classes of mammal: egg-laying mammals, known as Monotremes, which comprise just five species, all found in Australasia; and, of more relevance to the Peruvian Andes, mammals that give live birth. This second sub-class, the Theriiformes, can be further divided into two groups: marsupials or pouched mammals (Marsupialia) and placental mammals (Placentalia). The Peruvian Andes are home to many placental mammals, including carnivores, bats, insectivores, rodents, ungulates and primates. They are also home to opossums, which are South America's only marsupials.

Most Andean mammals are unobtrusive and hard to observe. Biologists who have worked for years in remote areas of the Andes proudly describe their few sightings of the larger species. In Inca times, when the human population was double what it is today, all animals enjoyed some form of protection – except during periodic hunts by the nobility. After the Spanish conquest, when the Inca infrastructure disintegrated, wild animals were hunted indiscriminately and suffered drastic population declines. These were exacerbated by the felling of the remaining High Andean woodlands, which provided essential cover for many animals. Today the persecution of mammals continues, in the case of some species because of the damage they do to crops, but more often because of ignorance. You should consider yourself lucky if you come across any of Peru's larger mammals on your travels. Nonetheless, there is still plenty to interest the careful observer.

PRIMATES

South America is richly endowed with primates, with over 120 species of monkey, tamarin and marmoset. New World monkeys (Callitrichidae) differ from Old World monkeys (Atelidae) in a number of ways. For one thing, their tails are prehensile, serving as fifth limbs while their owners forage for food in the canopy. In addition, their thumbs and big toes have become reduced as an adaptation to rapid travel in the treetops. They are also described as platyrrhine (flat-nosed), which refers to their having widely spaced, forward-facing nostrils – as opposed to the downward-facing nostrils of Old World monkeys, which are described as catarrhine.

None of the Peruvian primates can truly be said to live in the High Andes. This is mainly because they are arboreal animals that feed primarily on leaves, fruits and insects, so the cloud forest is the highest habitat to offer them suitable conditions. Nonetheless, a number of species do reach quite high elevations on the eastern slopes. These include the strictly nocturnal black-headed night monkey (*Aotus nigriceps*) with wide eyes, bold black-and-pale facial markings and a non-prehensile tail; the Andean or Rio Mayo titi monkey (*Callibebus oenanthe*), a very rare primate restricted to a small area near Moyobamba in north Peru; the robust common woolly monkey (*Lagothrix lagothrica*), which is easily seen in large groups in the cloud forest of Manu National Park; and the highly endangered yellow-tailed woolly

The common Woolly Monkey uses its prehensile tail as a fifth limb in the tree canopy. (RW)

monkey (*Lagothrix flavicauda*). The last of these is a dark reddish-brown primate with a yellow under-tail tip, which can still be seen in more isolated cloud forest areas of northern Peru – for example, around the ruins of Gran Pajaten, near Chachapoyas.

The only South American primates belonging to the catarrhine group are, of course, humans (*Homo sapiens*). Evidence suggests that the ancestors of the native human population arrived from North America, via the Panama isthmus, about 10,000 years ago. Technology and animal husbandry enabled humans to make a living above the treeline in the Peruvian High Andes. The fact that they did so suggests that the advantages of highland habitats outweighed the disadvantages sufficiently to make this a more attractive environment than those offered at lower altitudes. Since their arrival, humans have been as much a part of the natural history of the region as any other component. It can be argued that the critical point in their influence was the conquest of the mountains by the Spaniards in the 16th century, since that is when human activities began to fall seriously out of kilter with the natural world.

A Quechua farmer uses a traditional foot-plough, while his wife sows potato seeds. (HP)

UNGULATES

The word 'ungulate' means 'hoofed animal'. Ungulates comprise several groups of medium-sized to large herbivorous mammals that typically use the tips of their toes, that are usually hoofed, to sustain their entire body weight whilst they move. They are divided into two sub-orders: the even-toed ungulates (Artiodactyla) have two or four toes on each foot and include such groups as cattle, deer, pigs and llamas; the odd-toed ungulates (Perrisodactyla) have just one or three toes on each foot, and are represented by the horses, rhinos and tapirs.

CAMELIDS (LLAMAS AND RELATIVES)

The most conspicuous mammals encountered by a visitor to the Peruvian Andes are the camelids. As the name suggests, these are related to the familiar camels of the Old World. The best-known species are the domesticated llama (*Lama glama*) and alpaca (*Llama pacos*), which have served mountain people for centuries. However, two wild camelids also occur in the Peruvian Andes.

Llamas

Vicuña

Vicuña (*Vicugna vicugna*) are rather graceful camelids, standing just under a metre tall at the shoulder, with tawny-brown fur on the upperparts and longer, white fur on the throat and underside. They are reputed to have the finest wool of any living creature and, as a consequence, suffered decades of poaching and were brought to the brink of extinction. Poachers simply shot these fast and elusive animals, rather than struggling to trap them in the traditional way, and by 1964 their numbers had dwindled to just 12,000. Today they are on the increase again, thanks to the establishment of protected areas such as the Pampas Galeras Reserve in southern Peru, although conservationists still consider the species to be vulnerable.

In Inca times vicuña wool was harvested in a more responsible way. A yearly round-up, called *chaccu* in Quechua, marked the traditional corralling of hundreds of vicunas for their fine wool. Thousands of people would encircle the vicuña herds, chanting and shaking a long rope with colourful streamers in a time-honoured ritual, in which the animals were trapped, shorn of their wool and then released. Today, Peru holds a national *chaccu*, coupled with a three-day cultural festival, which is both a renewed expression of indigenous culture and a triumph for the international campaign to save these once endangered animals. Villages also conduct smaller-scale roundups throughout the May–September dry season.

The fine fur of the Vicuña has been its undoing. (HP)

Unlike llamas, the guanaco has never been domesticated. (HP)

Guanaco

The Guanaco (*Lama guanicoe*) is slightly larger than the vicuña, standing just over a metre at the shoulder, with a grey face, shorter ears and a characteristic wide-eyed appearance. Its colour varies from light brown to dark cinnamon, with paler-coloured fur on the underside, and is therefore easily distinguished from domesticated llamas and alpacas. This camelid reaches the northernmost limit of its range in central Peru and is found right down to Tierra del Fuego at the southern tip of the continent. In the Peruvian Andes you are most likely to encounter guanacos in the departments of Tacna, Moquegua and Arequipa, where they inhabit isolated rocky ravines with bunch grass. The exact relationship between domestic llamas and alpacas, and the wild gunacaos and vicunas is not clear. Some authorities state that all possible crosses of the four camelids have been acomplished and that the offspring of all crosses are fertile. Most taxonomists now agree that domestic llamas and alpacas are a result of cross-breeding of guanacos and vicunas. Whatever the relationship, the domesticated cameloids are to be found throughout the Peruvian highlands.

FROM BEAST OF BURDEN TO NOVO-ANDEAN CUISINE

The llama (pronounced *yaa-ma* and not to be confused with *lama*, which is a Tibetan Buddhist priest) occupies a special place in the history of the Andes. Up until the 16th century it was the largest domesticated animal in the region, before the Spanish introduced cattle, horses, donkeys and their hybrids. The llama served well as a pack animal along the intricate network of Inca highways, the *Quapac nan*, which were typically just wide enough for two llamas laden with cargo to pass each other comfortably. It was not really a beast of burden by European standards, however, being too slight in build. Nor was it a draught animal. The physical limitations of the llama and the generally difficult terrain meant that the wheel was never put to practical use by the Incas – or any other indigenous American population, north or south. However, the toughness and vigour of llamas in extreme conditions made them invaluable to the Incas. As well as carrying loads, they were a source of meat, milk, wool, bone, leather, gut and sinew. Even their droppings were used as fuel.

Andean woman spinning with alpaca wool (HP)

Today llamas are still very useful livestock in the Andes environment. The alpaca is rather smaller, but it has a bushy pelage that provides copious fine wool for the highland textile industry – the suri alpaca being the best breed. Its flesh is also very good: though scorned until recently by the middle classes as fit only for poor peasant farmers, alpaca steak is now a staple item on novo-Andean cuisine menus throughout the tourist towns of the region.

DEER

Other ungulates of the Andes include two large high-altitude grassland deer, which are among the more frequently seen animals in Peru. The Andean huemal (*Hippocamelus antisensis*), or *taruka* as it is known in Quechua, is the rarer of the two and now considered to be endangered. It is found at extremely high altitude, where its presence depends upon the availability of cover – mostly isolated patches of *Queuna* (*Polylepis*) woodland, which are increasingly threatened by a growing local need for firewood. This barrel-chested and short-legged species occurs in the Huascaran National Park and in isolated areas of the Cordillera Vilcanota. Its diagnostic Y-shaped antlers, each with two prongs, easily distinguish it from the white-tailed deer (*Odocoileus virginianus*), which has only a single prong but with several branches (or 'rack'). This latter species is common and well known to North American visitors since its range extends all the way to Canada. It tolerates human presence to an unusual degree and is the deer most likely to be seen by hikers in the Andes, especially on the Inca Trail.

The cloud forest also holds two smaller species of deer, both reportedly very shy and nocturnal. The authors have seen neither, despite working in the Manu National Park cloud forest for many years. The first is the dwarf brocket deer (*Mazama Chunyi*), which often reaches 3,200m elevation. This reddish-brown forest deer can be recognised by its small, rounded body, prominent eye-glands and the short, simple spike-like antlers. It often carries its hind quarters higher than its front quarters. The second is the similar-sized but darker brown northern pudu (*Pudu mephistophiles*), which ranges even higher, often to 4,000m or more. This species can be recognised by its very thin, delicate legs and short spike-like antlers.

TAPIR

The mountain tapir (*Tapirus pinchaque*) is a rare Andean cousin of the more familiar Brazilian tapir (*Tapir terrestris*) of the Amazon lowlands. Tapirs are odd-toed ungulates (Perissodactyla), which means they are more closely related to horses and rhinos than they are to even-toed ungulates (Artiodactyla) such as deer and camelids. They are characterised by their bulky, pig-like body and long rubbery snout, which they use to browse on foliage that would otherwise be out of reach. The mountain tapir inhabits the paramo and dwarf forest of extreme northern Peru, but is probably better looked for in Ecuador in locations such as Podocarpus National Park. Adults are a uniform sooty brown in colour, but calves are embellished with pale spots and stripes that imitate the dappled light on the forest floor, making it more difficult for predators to locate them.

Top Only male white-tailed deer have horns. (HP)

Middle The Andean huemal lives only at extremely high altitudes. (HP)

Above Encounters with mountain tapirs are rare and usually fleeting. (AL)

Young pampas cat (RW)

CARNIVORES

Carnivores (Carnivora) are meat-eaters, with claws and teeth designed for capturing and killing, and forward-facing eyes to help them judge speed and distance when hunting. There are five main families of carnivore in the neotropics, and all are well adapted to find, catch and kill a wide variety of animal prey.

CATS

Cats are territorial and generally solitary carnivores, each species specialised in hunting prey that suits its particular size. Most are largely nocturnal, which improves their hunting prowess and makes it easier for them to avoid humans. Consequently wild cats are seldom seen in the flesh, though you may find evidence of their presence in the form of footprints, droppings or the remains of a kill.

South America's only big cat, the jaguar (*Panthera onca*), inhabits the Amazonian lowlands and does not occur in the Andes. There are a variety of smaller felines though, that are occasionally seen. The largest is the puma (*Felis concolor*), also known in North America as cougar or mountain lion. This powerful, tawny cat weighs 45–75kg, though tends to be smaller in South America than in North

The puma is the most formidable predator in the Andes. (SCD/A)

Andean mountain cat stalks viscacha among the boulders.

America. It is unmarked, apart from distinctive dark face markings, and its sandy tones help it blend in with the rocks and bare earth so that it can better ambush prey. Pumas specialise in hunting deer, but they are opportunists that will take other mammals where available, including livestock. Once revered by the Incas as a symbol of power and elegance, they have since declined due to hunting pressure, and their habit of picking off an occasional unsuspecting llama or alpaca has not endeared them to Andean farmers. Today you might occasionally see this magnificent cat crossing a valley or hunting mountain viscachas in remoter areas.

Two smaller cats are also found in the Andes. Both are shy, with little known about their status and habits, and seeing either would count as a memorable Andean wildlife experience. The pampas cat (*Oncifelis colocolo*) is just over half a metre long and fairly catholic in its habitat requirements, ranging into inter-montane valleys, high grasslands and cloud forest up to 5,000m in elevation. Its prey consists mostly of guinea pigs and other similar-sized rodents, and ground-dwelling birds such as tinamous, and it will raid farms for poultry. The pampas cat was once killed for its skin, with 78,000 skins being exported from 1976–79. In 1980 they gained legal protection, so legal trading of their fur ceased.

The Andean mountain cat (*Oreailurus jacobita*) is rarer still and confined to treeless, rocky, semi-arid regions. It is slightly larger than a big domestic cat, growing up to 70cm in length, with a tail some 70% of its body length, and has exceptionally long fur. In Peru a specimen was once collected by a university expedition at an amazing 5,100m. above sea level. There is nothing in published literature about the habits of this cat, but the authors have observed one individual at 4,300m in the Cordillera Vilcanota stalking mountain viscachas on a scree slope, and have found tracks of others in the snow at similar altitudes.

Spectacled bear (HP)

SPECTACLED BEAR

The Andean or spectacled bear (*Tremarctos ornatus*) is the only member of its family found in South America. This small black bear gets its popular name from the creamy markings around its eyes. Females weigh about 65kg and males about 110kg. It is not particularly rare, but shuns human contact due to persecution from farmers and ranchers, so is seldom seen. It generally feeds on carrion, invertebrates, eggs and vegetable matter such as shoots, berries and roots, but will sometimes also take defenceless or injured animals. Andean bears are excellent tree climbers and often forage high in the branches. They are thought to play a vital role in plant dispersal by scattering seeds through their droppings.

The Andean bear has a poor reputation amongst small farmers due to its habit of raiding maize crops at the edge of cloud forests (the best place to spot one), and can cause significant economic damage to smallholders. The authors have heard repeated farmers' stories of bears

Each individual spectacled bear has unique facial markings. (RW)

attacking livestock, but we have been unable to confirm these and it seems unlikely. Its reputation, however, has caused the bear problems and it is still extensively hunted. Despite this, you can still see Andean bears along the Inca Trail and at Machu Picchu, and often along the road to the Manu National Park.

THE UKUKU AND THE SNOW STAR

The remote, ice-ringed Sinakara Valley high in Peru's southern Andes is usually a silent, lonely place inhabited only by alpacas. But, on the full moon before Corpus Christi (typically in early June), some 30,000 people gather upon the mountain slopes to celebrate the festival of the Snow Star at *Qoyllur Rit'i*. The Andean bear is important in Andean folklore and is called *Ukuku* in the native Quechua. Each group of native dancers at the festival has at least one *Ukuku* – a dancer in wool masks and shaggy tunics representing the bear. Although scores of different dance groups attend *Qoyllur Rit'i*, only the *Ukuku* accompanies nearly all groups and appears at no other festival. The *Ukuku* is a threshold being: a creature of dawn and dusk, whose habitat is the precarious edge between two worlds. He is a clown, a trickster and a policeman. He is also half-human, savage and appallingly strong. In this festival of chaos, he is the Lord of Misrule yet it is the *Ukuku* who protects the pilgrims from the perils of the *condenados* or damned souls who wander the glaciers at night and menace the living. And it is he who brings down the healing powers of the *Apu* in the form of glacier ice. In the Quechua legend of the *Ukuku*, the bear earns his manhood by defeating a *condenado* and becomes a model citizen. Thus the dancing of the *Ukuku* is traditionally a rite of passage performed by young males.

The South American fox often raids hen coops in rural areas. (HP)

SOUTH AMERICAN FOX

The dog family (Canidae) is represented in the Andes by the South American fox (*Pseudalopex culpaeus*), also known as *culpeo* – and locally as *zorro*. This is the largest South American fox species, and resembles the widely recognised red fox (*Vulpes vulpes*) of Europe, with a grey and reddish body, a white chin and reddish legs. It feeds on rodents, rabbits and hares, and is the main means of controlling the rabbit population that was introduced to South America in the early 1900s. It also sometimes takes very young lambs, up to a week old. However, its diet depends upon where it lives: in some areas it can be almost 97% carnivorous; in others, up to 30% of its diet is vegetable matter. This fox is a versatile species that occurs in many habitats and can be found up to 4,500m above sea level. Despite persecution, it remains common and is probably the most frequently seen large mammal in the Peruvian Andes.

COATI

The South American coati (*Nasua nasua*), also known as coatimundi, belongs to the raccoon family of carnivores (Procyonidae). It is primarily a lowland species, but also ranges into the Andes in Peru, where it inhabits the cloud forests of the humid eastern slopes. This distinctive animal has a long ringed tail and a flexible rubbery

The South American coati is common around Machu Picchu. (B/A)

snout. Like most of its family, it is omnivorous, feeding on a variety of invertebrates, as well as lizards, frogs, small rodents, eggs and some fruit. Unrelated females and their offspring often move around in large groups. They are easily seen at Machu Picchu, where they raid rubbish bins and other sources of discarded foodstuffs.

WEASELS, OTTERS AND SKUNKS

Weasels and their allies belong to the mustelid family (Mustelidae). These small to medium-sized carnivores mostly have short legs and long bodies. They are represented in the Peruvian Andes by a variety of species.

The long-tailed weasel (*Mustela frenata*) ranges all the way from Canada to northern Bolivia. With a long slender body, short legs and a bushy tail that is almost as long as the rest of its body, this weasel is an alert and agile predator on ground-nesting birds and rodents, stalking its prey by scent or sound, and then making a lightning attack which culminates in a deadly bite to the base of the skull. Weasels are active by day and night. They live in a variety of habitats, often in the mosaic of farms, hedgerows and stone walls, and have been recorded as high as 4,000m at Lake Junín.

Molina's hog-nosed skunk (*Conepatus chinga*) is found in areas of open vegetation and scrub forests. Like coatis, it is omnivorous, using its powerful claws and fleshy nose to root through the soil for insects and spiders. It will also feed on fruit, snakes, small mammals and eggs, its diet changing throughout the year according to the availability of food, with more insects being eaten in the spring and summer months. Skunks are most often seen crossing roads at night or, unfortunately, as road kills.

Top Neotropical otter (A/A)
Above Molina's hog-nosed skunk (B/A)

Similar in appearance is the greater grison (*Galactis vittata*). This ferret-sized predator has grizzled grey upperparts and black underparts, separated by a striking white band along the neck and across the forehead. It is found only in the Lake Titicaca basin area in the Peruvian Andes, where it feeds principally on small mammals such as viscachas and mice.

The only species of otter found in the Andes is the Neotropical river otter (*Lontra longicaudis*). This dark, glossy brown otter, with whitish fur on its underside, is fairly widespread, but rarely seen, and ranges up to 3,000m above sea level on the eastern slope of the Andes. It lives in clear water streams, where it feeds mainly on fish, crustaceans and molluscs. Its opportunist's diet also includes insects, small reptiles, birds and small mammals. One of the best places to observe otters is along the Urubamba River between Ollantaytambo and Machu Picchu.

Kangaroo rat (B/A)

RODENTS

Over 200 species of rodent (order Rodentia) have been recorded from the Peruvian Andes. These small to medium-sized herbivorous mammals have adapted to fill most niches that the environment has to offer. Many do well at high altitude: their thick pelts provide good insulation, and they can escape the elements by digging burrows underground – often with complex chambers and networks of interconnecting tunnels. Rodents as a group are characterised by having perpetually growing incisor teeth that are constantly worn down by their gnawing habits, as they feed on tough plant matter such as bark, tubers, roots, stems, seeds and nuts. They are also notorious for their ability to multiply rapidly in favourable conditions. At high altitudes many species are diurnal, allowing them to avoid the freezing conditions at night, and can often be seen scurrying along walls. Although rodents may sometimes seem rather uninteresting animals, they are a vital component of the ecosystem, providing food for predatory birds and mammals, and helping to disperse the seeds of plants. The following account describes a few of the better-known species in the Peruvian Andes.

PORCUPINES

Porcupines are large and unusual rodents. Those found in South America belong to the prehensile-tailed porcupine family (Erethizontidae), otherwise known as *coendous* from their genus name *Coendou*. These cat-sized animals are well adapted to arboreal life, with a prehensile tail that curls around branches like a fifth limb while the animal climbs and forages. The rest of the animal is covered in modified hairs: those against the skin are bristly, but the ones above have evolved into protective spines or quills, equipped with very sharp tips that break off in the flesh of an attacker and cause wounds to turn septic. One species that ranges into the Andes is the Brazilian porcupine (*Coendou prehensilis*).

RATS AND MICE

By far the majority of rodents in Peru belong in this family, the Muridae, which comprises several subfamilies in the region. The Abrocomidae includes the chinchilla rats and giant tree rats, which are relatively large, semi-arboreal animals.

The Cricetidae comprise the New World or native rats and mice, which are similar to true rats and mice. The Echymyidae are the spiny and bamboo rats, characterised by the bristly hairs on their backs. And the Heteromyidae contains the pocket mice and kangaroo rats, which are generally small, with rear limbs adapted for leaping. In this last group perhaps the most intriguing species is the Cusco chinchilla rat (*Cuscomys ashaninka*). This powerfully built animal is the size of a small domestic cat, with large claws and a white streak running from its head to its snout. It was discovered only in 1999, and even then only because a long-tailed weasel happened to have just killed the type specimen prior to being disturbed by mammologist Dr Louise Emmons of the Smithsonian Institution. Scientists now believe that this species might well be the so-called Inca tomb rat, which is thought to have been kept as a pet by the Incas – its skeleton having been found alongside those of its owners in graves at Machu Picchu.

CAVIES AND THEIR ALLIES

The cavies are robust rodents with stocky torsos, short legs and, typically, vestigial tails. Four families fall into this category, of which the Caviidae is the family to which the domestic guinea pig (*Cavia porcellus*) belongs. The Incas originally reared this animal for its meat, centuries before it entered the worldwide pet trade. Today it no longer exists in the wild, having been domesticated by selective breeding and hybridisation. However, two wild cavy species still live in the Peruvian Andes. The first is the montane guinea pig (*Cavia tschudii*), which is found mostly in moist habitats with scattered rocks and thick vegetation – where it makes its runways – ranging up to 3,800m elevation. This species can regularly be seen at the Hucarapay Lakes, just south of Cusco. The similar yellow-toothed cavy (*Galea musteloides*) is found only in the Lake Titicaca basin. Closely related to cavies is the mountain paca (*Agouti taczanowskii*). This larger rodent inhabits the cloud forests, and skulls have been reported from burial caves at Machu Picchu.

The Brazilian porcupine is at home in the branches or on the ground. (MP)

PET, LAB ANIMAL OR LUNCH?

When Europeans first arrived in South America, they found cavies kept as domesticated animals by local people from what is now northwestern Venezuela to central Chile. Traders subsequently brought *Cavia porcellus* to Europe, where the animal assumed the name guinea pig due to a popular misconception that it hailed from Guinea. This species no longer exists in the wild, but domesticated guinea pigs are now found worldwide in captivity. They are strictly herbivorous, with a diet in captivity that consists typically of commercial pellets, fruits and vegetables – especially green leaves such as carrot tops and lettuce.

The guinea pig has served as a food source for centuries in Ecuador, Peru and Bolivia. It makes a traditional dish known as *cuy*, which dates back at least fifteen centuries to pre-Incan times and has been served on special occasions ever since. A painting of the last supper in Cusco Cathedral depicts Christ eating guinea pig; it would have been inconceiveable to the painter that he would have eaten anything else at such an important meal. Care and preparation of the guinea pig used to be seen as a woman's chore, but raising guinea pigs is increasingly becoming a commercial practice, especially with the recent surge in tourism. *Cuy* now appears on the menu of many restaurants in the highland regions, though you may be able to sample it more cheaply from street stalls at a local festival. It comes either fried or baked, prepared with *huacartay* (an aromatic Andean herb), cumin and garlic, and is served whole (head, paws and all) on a platter with potatoes and vegetables. It tastes a little like chicken, but with a gamey flavour all its own. There is seldom much meat on a guinea pig; eating one is an art form – and one which the authors have been happy to perfect!

Guinea pigs have also been an invaluable resource in laboratories, used for research in fields such as nutrition, pathology, genetics, toxicology, the isolation of bacteria and the production of serum. They also make excellent pets, with some show-quality breeds being worth thousands of dollars.

Domesticated guinea pig (HP)

Mountain viscachas are fond of sunbathing in the late afternoon. (HP)

CHINCHILLAS AND VISCACHAS

The *Chinchillidae* family comprises the chinchillas and viscachas. These are generally considered to be among the 'cuter' rodents, with their large eyes, silky pelts and bushy tails. Their exceptionally fine and dense fur is an adaptation to alpine conditions, providing excellent insulation from chilling winds. Unfortunately there is also a great human demand for this fur, and numbers of these rodents have been greatly depleted by fur traders. The short-tailed chinchilla (*Chinchilla brevicaudata*), which was once found in the highlands of southern Peru, has not been recorded for over 50 years and is now thought to be extinct in the country. Viscachas, however, remain common, and colonies can be seen on most trekking routes throughout the Peruvian Andes. There are two species in Peru, the southern viscacha (*Lagidium viscacha*) and the mountain viscacha (*Lagidium peruanum*). The latter is the more commonly seen, usually on rocky slopes where small groups may sun themselves in the early morning or late afternoon sun. They blend in well with their background – you can often be staring straight at one without seeing it until it moves.

The Andean hairy armadillo, like all its kind, will roll into a ball for protection. (B/A)

OTHER SMALL MAMMALS

Here we mention, for completeness, a mixed bag of mammals that can be seen in the Peruvian Andes. Armadillos, shrews and mouse possums are rarely seen and it is the larger white-eared opossum that is most likely to be encountered.

ARMADILLOS

Armadillos are known as edentates, which literally means 'toothless', although they do have poorly developed teeth. They belong to the order Xenarthra, which is almost entirely confined to South and Central America. These excavation specialists use all four, heavily clawed limbs to dig burrows and unearth their food, which includes ants and termites, as well as any other invertebrates and small vertebrates they may come across. Their backs are armoured against attack from predators in a similar way to tortoises, except that their armour comprises rows of articulated plates, which are modified hairs. Several species occur in the Peruvian Andes and they are essentially similar in all respects except size. The Andean hairy armadillo (*Chaetophractus nationi*) in the southern altiplano is about 50cm in length and furnished with long hairs for insulation, which even protrude from between the carapace plates. This species has the curious habit of burrowing under, and even inside, large carcasses to get at the maggots and grubs of putrefactive insects. The hairy long-nosed armadillo (*Dasypus pilosus*) also occurs in the south-central Andes of Peru.

HARES AND RABBITS

Rabbits and hares are not rodents, but belong to a separate order of mammals, called lagomorphs (Lagomorpha). The only rabbit native to Peru is the Brazilian cottontail (*Sylvilagus brasiliensis*), but this does not range above elevations of 2,500m. The brown hare (*Lepus eropeaeus*) is a European species that was introduced into the altiplano areas of the southern Andes centuries ago. It now lives in a feral state and may be seen in the high country of the south.

SHREWS

Shrews (Soricomorpha) look superficially like rodents, but are actually insectivores and belong to an entirely different order. Insectivores are not well represented in the Peruvian Andes, with the least shrew (*Cryptotis peruviensis*), found in the department of Cajamarca, being the only species. This tiny mammal, just a few centimetres long, feeds upon small invertebrates, small reptiles and carrion. It leads a typically high-octane shrew life, needing to eat its own bodyweight, or thereabouts, in food each day just to stay alive.

MARSUPIALS

Although Australia is famously the home of marsupials, South America has a surprising number of its own. These fall into the 'magnorder' Ameridelphia – as distinct from the Australidelphia, which are the Australasian marsupials.

Marsupials use pouches in which to nurture their young, which are born at a very early stage in foetal development. There are seven genera in the region. Different species vary in size, but all follow a similar general design, with rodent-like bodies, and prehensile tails and opposable big toes as adaptations to climbing in trees (though they are equally at home on the ground). Their heads resemble those of hedgehogs, as they are essentially marsupial insectivores, having claimed ecological niches in the virtual absence of true insectivores.

Opossums and mouse-opossums

Opossums are well known for their multiple births of 10–14 babies and the way in which mothers subsequently carry their offspring bunched on their backs. The common and often seen white-eared opossum (*Didelphis albiventris*) is a habitat generalist and omnivore. It is adapted to fluctuating conditions of rainfall, humidity,

Opossum suckling its many young (HP)

Common long-tongued bat (RNB/A)

and temperature, and is found in various montane habitats, from open areas and mountains to deciduous forest. The Peruvian Andes are also home to many species of mouse-opossum (*Marmosa* spp.). These are small and mouse-like, ranging from 85–185mm in length, and have dark gray to brown upperparts, with paler underparts. They give birth typically to 6–10 babies, but little else is known of their ecology.

Shrew-opossums

Shrew opossums are small animals with small eyes and a thick, grey or grey-brown pelage, which look practically identical to true shrews. This is because they display a phenomenon known as convergent evolution, whereby two groups of unrelated creatures adapt similar characteristics in order to fill similar ecological niches. What is most irregular, though, is that this usually happens in corresponding habitats in different places, so that the two groups never naturally meet. However, the true shrews arrived from North America several thousand years ago when the Central American isthmus was formed, so that both groups now live alongside one another and are presumably competing for the exact same resources. The shrew opossums of this region belong to a single genus, *Lestoros*, with the Peruvian shrew opossum (*Lestoros inca*) being the only known species in the Peruvian Andes. It is nocturnal and restricted to the south of the country.

BATS

The natural history and exact distribution of Peruvian bats (order Chiroptera) is poorly known. What we currently know is that more than sixty species have been recorded in the Peruvian Andes, falling into four families and around thirty genera. This variety reflects the number of niches offered by the differences in altitude, climate and vegetation. Consequently there are species adapted for particular diets, so that some are fruit-eaters, while others eat pollen and nectar. Many are insectivorous though, hunting mostly airborne insects. A few catch invertebrates – and even small vertebrates, such as reptiles – in trees or on the ground, whilst others have mixed or omnivorous diets.

Most bats are unlikely to be seen at all simply because they only come out after dark. During daylight hours they typically roost in all kinds of discreet hiding places – beneath roofs, behind shutters, in caves, between crevices, down tunnels, under tree bark and so on. Individual species are very difficult to identify: most appear superficially very similar to one another, and the situation is further complicated by the fact that many do not yet have common names. However, all is not lost! With perseverance and a good flashlight you are most likely to find several species of the *Pyllostomatidae* family, also known as the New World leaf-nosed bats, during night walks. Those most commonly encountered in the cloud forests of Junín, Pasco, Huanuco, Ayacucho and Cusco include the common long-tongued bat (*Glossophaga sorcina*), hairy-legged long-tongued bat (*Anoura geoffroyi*), short-tailed nectar bat (*Anoura caudifer*) and blackish long-tongued bat (*Anoura brevirostrum*). All these species are small, with narrow muzzles, short 'nose-leaves' and small ears, but their most remarkable feature is their extraordinary extendable tongue, which has evolved to reach deep into flowers for nectar. The bats are essential pollinators of certain plants, whose long tube-like flowers open only to release their musky odours at night. The length of each species' tongue has evolved to fit the particular plant upon which it feeds. Two fruit-eating species you are most likely to encounter in the cloud forests of southern Peru are the Manu short-tailed bat (*Carollia manu*) and silvery fruit-eating bat (*Dermanura glauca*).

Other common bat species of higher cloud forest habitats include those belonging to the vesper bat family (*Vespertilionidae*), such as the big-eared brown bat (*Histiotus macrotus*), the Brazilian brown bat (*Eptesicus brasiliensis*), the hairy-legged myotis (*Myotis keaysi*) and the Montane myotis (*Myotis oxyotus*). These vesper bats are small to medium-sized species that are very agile and rapid flyers, and use their large tail membrane as a scoop to help trap flying insects.

Mountain viscacha (see page 69) (PO)

BIRDS

Andean condor (PH/D)

South America holds almost one third of all bird species found on earth, including many endemics, and Peru, with over 1,850 species recorded, has the second highest number of any single country after Colombia. It is thus in the world of birds that the Peruvian Andes really shine as a wildlife destination. With such a mega-diversity – from the multi-coloured tanagers, hummingbirds, toucans and parrots, to the many elusive inhabitants of mossy cloud forest – even the most casual observer cannot but wonder at them.

The distribution of different species depends on their habitat requirements, which in turn reflects their preferred food source. In the Andes there is little long-distance migration, since most of the region lies within the tropics, so birds do not need to travel far to find food during winter. Local movements, however, may be triggered by a sudden abundance of food, such as fruiting trees for toucans. There is also some altitudinal migration (from highland to lowlands). So, except for a few migrants from North America that reach the northern Peruvian Andes during the boreal winter, and a few ground-tyrants that make it to the central Peruvian Andes during the austral winter, the bird life of the Andes is similar all year round.

Birds are distinguished as a class from all other vertebrates by one unique attribute: feathers. These replaced scales during an evolutionary process that began more than 130 million years ago as birds evolved from reptiles. They have since diversified into an extraordinary variety, and today taxonomists classify them within three broad groups: non-passerines, sub-oscine passerines and oscine passerines. The term 'passerine' is derived from *Passer*, the scientific name for the humble sparrow. Passerines are technically defined by the structure of their feet, which have three toes directed forwards and one toe directed backwards that joins the leg at the same level as the others. They are also sometimes called 'perching birds'. Oscine passerines comprise a huge number of families and species all over the world. Sub-oscine passerines comprise several families that occur mostly in tropical America and are defined by a structural difference in their voice organs. Non-passerines are, by definition, non-perching birds, and comprise a mixed bag of different orders.

NON-PASSERINES
RHEAS AND TINAMOUS
The largest bird in the Andes is the puna rhea (*Rhea tarapacencis*). This huge flightless species is the South American equivalent of the ostrich and is now quite rare due to hunting by man for its eggs and meat. It inhabits the extreme high Andean plateau or altiplano. With luck, you may see rheas running across the plains in the highlands of extreme southwest Peru, or better still in the Parque Nacional Lauca in northern Chile.

Tinamous also inhabit the highland plains. Though certainly not restricted to the high Andean altiplano, they are conspicuous here, and the whistles of the ornate tinamou (*Nothoprocta ornata*) or Darwin's nothura (*Nothura darwini*) are often heard from deep in the tall *Ichu* grass as the birds feed amongst herds of llamas and alpacas. Tinamous are called *perdiz* in Spanish (meaning partridge), after the first Spanish conquerors' observation that they resembled Old World partridges. They

The Andean tinamou skulks in dense *ichu* grass and is more often heard than seen. (RW)

are furtive ground-dwelling birds that hide by crouching and sitting, flushing in an explosive manner only when almost stepped upon. Most Andean species are polygamous, with two or more females laying eggs in the same scrape. Some species are also found in the cloud forests, though here they are almost exclusively heard, not seen. These include the hooded tinamou (*Nothocercus nigrocapillus*) and tawny-breasted tinamou (*Nothocercus Julius*). The call of the former is a common sound of the cloud forests of the Manu Biosphere Reserve. In the farmland mosaic of the inter-montane valleys, the Andean tinamou (*Nothoprocta pentlandii*) and curve-billed tinamou (*Nothoprocta curvirostris*) are perhaps the easiest to see. In Incan times tinamous were domesticated for their meat and eggs, before the Spaniards introduced the now ubiquitous domesticated chicken.

Top Short-winged grebe (RW)
Middle Junín grebe (HP)
Above Immature Andean goose (HP)

WATER BIRDS
Flightless grebes
A conspicuous element of the High Andes is the number of lakes, including enormous bodies of water such as Lake Titicaca and Lake Junín. Both these lakes are home to flightless grebes, whose flightlessness is an evolutionary adaptation to the absence of natural predators. Lake Titicaca has the short-winged grebe (*Rollandia microptera*), aptly named for its underdeveloped wings. This species is fairly common, and often seen by visitors around the Floating Islands of the Uros Indians, or on the way to more remote islands such as Amantani, Taquile and Suasi. Lake Junín (called *Chinchaycocha* and revered by the Incas) is less frequently visited and home to the endemic Junín flightless grebe (*Podiceps taczanowskii*), named after the early Polish zoologist Wladyslaw Taczanowski, who wrote one of the first works on Peruvian ornithology. This species is threatened with extinction due to lake pollution from nearby mining concerns: fewer than 350 pairs are thought to remain. Fortunately conservation groups are showing a great interest in its fate and mining companies, conscious of their environmental image, are now helping to protect it. The extinct Colombian grebe (*Podiceps andinus*) was not so lucky. An exhaustive search in 1981 of its only remaining location, Lake Tota near Bogota, failed to find any left. Its demise was probably due to habitat loss during the late 1950s, when the lake's water level was reduced for irrigation.

Other lake waterfowl
As well as the big lakes, there are thousands of smaller bodies of water that are all home to abundant waterfowl. Among these the birdwatcher will encounter a variety of ducks (Anatidae): puna teal (*Anas puna*) is distinguished by its white cheeks and cobalt

blue bill; crested duck (*Anas specularoides*), found mostly at high altitude, by its floppy crest and large size; and cinnamon teal (*Anas cyanoptera*), by its pretty chestnut plumage. Yellow-billed pintail (*Anas goergica*), speckled teal (*Anas flavirostris*) and Andean duck (*Oxyura ferruginea*) are also common. The ducks are often accompanied by large groups of Andean coots (*Fulica ardesiac*) and common moorhens (*Gallinula chloropus*), both members of the rail family – though they superficially resemble ducks and live on aquatic vegetation. Sometimes a few neotropic cormorants (*Phalacrocorax brasilianus*) are also present, distinguished from ducks by their long slim necks and low carriage in the water. The only goose in the Peruvian Andes is the Andean goose (*Chloephaga melanoptera*), which is often seen on the highest lakes and their surrounding flooded fields and wet areas. Known as *Huallata* in the Quechua language, this largely black-and-white species is important in Andean folklore, and at an isolated community near Cusco there is an annual traditional dance that imitates its mating display.

Torrent duck

One duck you will not find on Andean lakes is the torrent duck (*Merganetta armata*). This inhabitant of rushing rivers and streams is adapted to feeding in the fast-flowing waters that cascade down the mountainsides – a niche that it has claimed all to itself. Torrent ducks seldom stray any real distance from their streams and even nest in crevices between waterside boulders. They feed primarily on aquatic invertebrates, and are a common sight on the Urubamba River – visible from the train that takes visitors to Machu Picchu.

A female torrent duck contemplates taking the plunge. (HP)

Top Andean gull (HP)
Above Andean lapwing (HP)

Waders

Lakes and wetlands are also home to many waders (shorebirds), either permanently or as stopovers for migrants. During April–May and August–October, their shorelines are crammed with migrating waders passing between their breeding grounds in the tundra of North America and their wintering grounds in southern South America. These include greater and lesser yellowlegs (*Tringa melanoleuca/flavipes*), Baird's sandpiper (*Calidris bairdii*) and American golden plover (Pluvialis dominica). Breeding residents include the pretty Andean lapwing (*Vanellus resplendens*), called *Leke-leke* in Quechua, and the harder to see puna plover, puna snipe and Andean avocet. For birdwatchers, the most sought-after species is the diademed sandpiper plover (*Phegornis mitchellii*), which lives exclusively on high Andean bogs, such as those at Marcopomacocha, along the central highway above Lima. This is an intricately patterned bird with a downcurved bill. The Andean gull (*Larus serranus*) is also often found in large colonies in these environments, and is recognisable by its contrasting black head in the breeding season.

Seedsnipes are closely related to waders, but are found in drier grassland habitats. They resemble Old World sandgrouse and live in flocks on the high puna grasslands and scree slopes. Locally called *Agachonas* from their habit of crouching (*agachar* in Spanish), they are said to be unlucky: one landing near your house is traditionally held to foretell a death.

Flamingos

The high saline lakes of the Andes are home to three of the world's five species of flamingo. This harsh, windswept environment, with not a palm tree or beach to be seen, rather contradicts the tropical holiday image of these birds. The Andes are home to the Chilean flamingo (*Phoenicopterus chilensis*), Andean flamingo (*Phoenicoparrus andinus*) and the puna or James's flamingo (*Phoenicoparrus jamesi*). The last of these is the rarest, although concentrations of up to 25,000 birds can be seen at Bolivia's Laguna Colorado. In Peru large numbers of flamingos also gather at Laguna Salinas in the highlands, northeast of the southern city of Arequipa, when the water levels are suitable.

The pinkish colouring of flamingo plumage is derived from the planktonic diatoms (microscopic algae) that form their staple diet. This food is seldom available for birds in captivity, which receive dietary supplements to prevent their plumage from reverting to white. Flamingos are unique among birds in feeding with

Chilean flamingo (MDA)

their bills upside down, sieving diatoms from the water in much the same way that baleen whales filter zooplankton from the oceans. They are colonial nesters, often in colonies of thousands. This is partly because the food supply for chicks is concentrated within the confines of particular lakes. But living en masse also increases the chicks' chances of escaping predators, which find it more difficult to operate in the confusion of a crowd.

Herons and ibis

Herons (Ardeidae) are familiar birds to most people, with their long necks, long legs and dagger-like bills. They are typically seen near water, often standing patiently in wait for fish and other aquatic prey or wading through the shallows.

The two most common species of heron in the Peruvian Andes are the snowy egret (*Egretta thula*), a medium-sized white heron, with black bill and legs, and bright yellow feet, and the much larger great egret (*Ardea alba*), also white, but with black legs and big yellow bill. Along fast-flowing Andean rivers such as the Rio Urubamba in southern Peru, you may also see the much sought-after fasciated tiger heron (*Tigrisoma fasciatum*), which is easily recognisable by its heavily banded neck and upper body, but is a nervous bird and will flush easily upon approach.

Another common wading bird you are most likely to encounter is the puna ibis (*Plegadis ridgwayi*). This large, purplish-brown bird has glossy purplish-green 'highlights', glossy green wings and tail, a dark chestnut head and neck, and long black legs. It is most often found around Andean lakes and other water bodies, and also on recently ploughed fields, where large groups forage with a characteristic slow walk, probing the ground with their long, curved bills.

Puna ibis (RW)

The Andean condor has the largest wing area of any bird. (HP)

BIRDS OF PREY

Birds of prey are numerous and conspicuous in the Andes, which largely reflects the accessibility of their main food supply, rodents. At lower altitudes rodents are primarily nocturnal creatures, foraging at night in order to evade predators. But in the High Andes, especially on the open grasslands and altiplano, most species are diurnal, preferring to spend the cold nights snug in their underground burrows or crevices. This is to the decided advantage of the falcons, hawks and eagles that feed on them.

The widespread Aplomado falcon (*Falco femoralis*) often hunts in pairs. Like most falcons, it has pointed wings and a tapering tail as an adaptation for capturing prey in flight, where speed is the key to success. In South and Central America, however, the falcon family also includes an atypical group of raptors known as caracaras, which occupy a similar niche to that occupied by crows and ravens in temperate countries. The mountain caracara (*Phalcoboenus megalopterus*) is one such species. It has taken the role of scavenger and opportunist, being omnivorous in its diet and often found near human habitation.

Hawks and eagles have rounded wings with long tails and legs. They are adapted to hunting prey on the ground or amongst foliage, where manoeuvrability is essential. On the high puna and altiplano even the most casual observer can see large hawks, such as the puna hawk (*Buteo poecilochrous*), black-chested buzzard eagle (*Geranoaetus melanoleucus*) and red-backed hawk (*Buteo polyosoma*). These birds of prey are conspicuous and abundant, and – along with the cinereous harrier (*Circus cinereus*) – can easily be seen from the tourist train on the way from Cusco to Puno or around Lake Titicaca.

Up at the treeline, birds of prey are somewhat scarcer and harder to see. The cloud forest is home to small hawks, such as the white-throated hawk (*Buteo albigula*) and white-rumped hawk (*Buteo leuchorrous*). The mighty black-and-chestnut eagle (*Oroaetus isidori*) and solitary eagle (*Harpyhaliaetus solitarius*) can also be seen in the cloud forest of the Manu Biosphere Reserve, and even sometimes at Machu Picchu. These latter two are fully capable of capturing a woolly monkey, where troops of these primates occur.

Mountain caracaras occupy the niche of scavengers in the absence of crows. (RW)

Andean condor

The only vulture to occur in the Andes is the huge Andean condor, which has become emblematic of the region. Like all vultures, this bird is a scavenger, with a naked head and short bill designed for eating carrion. It nests on inaccessible rocky cliffs, where it soars with great proficiency, using keen eyesight to spot carrion far below. New World vultures, unlike Old World vultures, are not technically birds of prey: they have chicken-like feet that are incapable of grasping or killing. Nonetheless condors are impressive by their sheer size: this massive bird has a wingspan of over 3m and weighs up to 11kg.

IMMORTAL BIRD OF THE INCAS

The Andean condor, or *kuntur* as it is known in Quechua, has long been a source of myth and legend in the Andes. The Incas believed it to be immortal, representing strength and intelligence, and that it lifted the sun over the mountains each day. It was also believed to make predictions – both good and bad. Legend says that the death of a condor that fell from the sky during the Inti Raymi Sun Festival (still held today at the fortress of Sacsayhuaman near Cusco on the day of the winter equinox), foretold the destruction of the empire a year before the Spanish conquerors arrived. The truth is less glamorous: the condor, majestic though it may appear, is simply a vulture that feds on dead flesh. Every year one or two sensational stories in the less discerning newspapers tell of a condor snatching away an unguarded infant while the mother was watching her flock of llamas. This is a physical impossibility, as the condor cannot grasp or lift prey with its feet. As a footnote, 'El Condor Pasa', a song made famous by Simon and Garfunkel in the 1960s and to be heard in every Peruvian tourist restaurant, is actually a typical Inca dance, based on authentic Incan folk melodies. Around 1916, Peruvian composer Daniel Alomia Robles notated this popular traditional melody and used it as the basis for an instrumental suite.

The Yungas pygmy owl may hunt by daylight on overcast days. (Al/A).

NOCTURNAL BIRDS

Several species of owl and nightjar are found in the Peruvian Andes. These birds all hunt at night, trusting to their cryptic camouflage patterning to avoid detection by day. Owls vary from the large eared Magellanic horned owl (*Bubo magellanicus*) of rocky outcrops such as the Sacred Valley of the Incas, to the tiny pygmy owls (*Glaucidium* sp.) and screech owls (*Megascops* sp.) of the cloud forests. Owls often use the old nesting holes of woodpeckers, as they are not furnished with the necessary excavating equipment themselves. The size of each species determines what kind of hole it will use and also the kinds of prey it prefers. Screech owls will take small mammals, songbirds and lizards, while pygmy owls specialise in large invertebrates, such as flying insects and worms. Owls typically swallow their prey whole. The indigestible parts of animals, such as bones, feathers, fur and chitin (the exoskeletons of insects) are eventually regurgitated in the form of pellets.

Nightjars are insect eaters, which use their huge gapes and aerial agility to trap their prey in flight. The males of some species, such as the swallow-tailed nightjar (*Uropsalis segmentata*) of the higher cloud forest edge or the lyre-tailed nightjar (*Uropsalis lyra*) of the lower cloud forest habitats, have spectacular tails that are elaborately elongated for aerial courtship displays.

WOODPECKERS

Woodpeckers are famed for their ability to chisel away at tree trunks using their bills. Their especially thick skulls enable them to absorb the shock from each blow and so prevent injury to the brain. They use their bills to find food, create nest sites and communicate. The last they achieve by 'drumming' their bill loudly against a hollow branch during the spring courtship display. Woodpeckers can detect the likely presence of wood-boring beetle and moth larvae by listening for the hollow note of their tunnels and chambers when striking at a branch or tree trunk. They then chisel away until they enter the cavity, employing their tongue to find and remove the morsel of food. Woodpeckers' tongues are uniquely rooted at the top of the skull, enabling them to extend far beyond the end of the bill. They are also equipped with barbed tips and gluey saliva, enabling the birds to catch their prey more easily.

Cloud forest woodpeckers include the bar-bellied woodpecker (*Veniliornis nigriceps*) and the pretty crimson-mantled woodpecker (*Piculus rivolii*). But the most enigmatic woodpecker doesn't live in trees at all: the Andean flicker (*Colaptes rupicola*) lives on the high grasslands and plains, making its home in earth banks and old adobe buildings.

THE WOODPECKER THAT HELPED THE INCA

There is a popular myth among Andean peasant farmers that goes something like this. When the first Inca decided he wanted to build temples in honour of the sun-god Inti, he realised he did not know how to cut the stone, so he commanded all the members of the animal kingdom to appear before him. 'Which of you can help me cut the stone?' asked the Inca king of the animals before him. The animals, including the puma and the bear, looked at one another and shook their heads. Then, from about nine rows back, the Jacachu (as the Andean flicker is known in Quechua) piped up, saying: 'I can help, great Inca, but it will take me a few days.' With that, the flicker flew off the top of the Andes and down into the Amazon rainforest, reappearing a few days later with a seed. 'Oh great Inca,' said the flicker, 'plant this seed and a bush will grow. Take the leaves from the bush, then grind them into a paste with water and spread the paste upon the stone you wish to cut. The paste will soften the stone so that you can cut it.' This, the Inca did, and he proceeded to build all the Inca cities and constructions whose ruins we see today.

The Andean flicker often excavates holes in old adobe buildings. (HP)

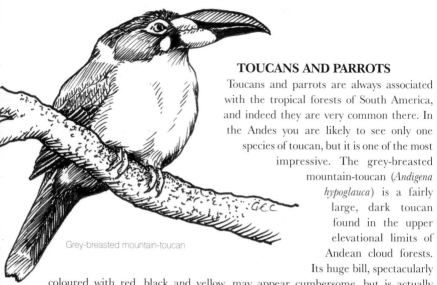

TOUCANS AND PARROTS

Toucans and parrots are always associated with the tropical forests of South America, and indeed they are very common there. In the Andes you are likely to see only one species of toucan, but it is one of the most impressive. The grey-breasted mountain-toucan (*Andigena hypoglauca*) is a fairly large, dark toucan found in the upper elevational limits of Andean cloud forests. Its huge bill, spectacularly coloured with red, black and yellow, may appear cumbersome, but is actually extremely lightweight and versatile. It enables the toucan to reach a wide variety of foodstuffs, from fruits and berries to invertebrates and small mammals, while perched in the branches of trees. This cavity-nesting bird is now an endangered species due to the deforestation of its habitat. Despite this, however, it is readily seen by visitors hiking the Inca trail to Machu Picchu, or along the Manu road in southern Peru and in the Carpish Mountains of central Peru.

Grey-breasted mountain-toucan

Parrots

Although parrots are popularly associated with hot steaming jungle, some species are found high in the mountains. Andean and mountain parakeets (*Bolborhynchus orbygnesius* and *aurifrons*) reach almost to the snowline on occasions, and both mitred and scarlet-fronted parakeets (*Aratinga mitrata* and *wagleri*) occur in cloud forests and inter-montane valleys. Parakeets can be noisy and conspicuous, with their green and red plumage, but disappear as if by magic when they land in a tree crown. To differentiate them from the general parrot order (Psittaciformes), they are defined as small birds with long, graduated tails and predominantly green plumage. Being small, they can cope better than larger species with relatively sparse food supplies. They also adapt readily to human-modified landscapes, and sometimes even gain reputations as crop-raiding pests.

Mitred parakeet (HS)

Parakeets, like toucans, have zygodactyl feet, which means two toes pointing forwards and two backwards on each foot. As well as giving the birds excellent climbing abilities, these feet double as 'hands' to hold items of food while the birds manipulate them with their powerful, hooked bills. Parakeets are highly social birds, so they move in flocks and keep in constant noisy communication with one another. They also nest communally, which helps with protection from predators, because having so many pairs of eyes helps them spot danger quickly and react to it en masse. Other montane species of parrot include the speckle-faced parrot (*Pionus tumultuosus*) and scaly-naped parrot (*Amazona mercenaria*), both of which have robust bodies and short, square tails.

BIRD DIVERSITY AT MACHU PICCHU

Machu Picchu and its associated archaeological sites along the Inca Trail have long been protected as part of the Machu Picchu Historical Sanctuary. Little did its creators know that they were also protecting some of the richest bird habitat in the Americas. Here, in an area of only 32,590ha, over 420 species of bird have already been recorded and a further 40 or so are expected to appear as research continues. Many are declining or threatened elsewhere due to the destruction of their habitat. It is thus fortunate that this archaeological sanctuary also protects precious habitat – intact montane and elfin forest, and fragmented *Polylepis* patches – which produces its wonderful avian diversity. Machu Picchu is on the eastern slope of the Andes, where montane forest drops away towards the Amazon Basin. The lowland forest holds the highest count of bird species that can be found in one place. However, the slopes of the Andes are richer in species over a more extensive area: 1,000 can be found along a 200km transect from the High Andean grasslands down the eastern slope of the Andes to the Amazon lowlands. This is about the same as throughout the whole of the Amazon Basin.

The area is also well known for the high incidence of endemism and near-endemism among birds, plants and other organisms (an endemic species being one that exists nowhere else). This is probably due to its unique topography. Most of the Andean slope inclines directly towards the Amazon lowlands, but at Machu Picchu the area between the Mapacho and Apurimac rivers forms a large fan of projective mountain ridges, separated by deep valleys. Machu Picchu is perched above the Urumbamba River, which separates the Cordillera Vilcanota from the Cordillera Vilcabamba. These high mountain ridges, with peaks reaching 6,000m, provide excellent protection from cold southern winds, known as *friajes*, during the southern winter. They thus offer an ecological stability that is commonly consistent with high levels of endemism. The area's endemic birds probably represent relict populations that were able to withstand extreme climatic variations in the past, due to this protective topography. They subsequently played an important role in the evolution of Andean avifauna.

PIGEONS AND DOVES

Pigeons and doves (family Columbidae) are the only birds able to draw water up into their mouths: others must fill their beaks and tip them back to swallow. This enables them to drink their fill very quickly, and so minimises their chances of capture by a predator. Most species are grain-eaters, which can result in some being seen as crop pests – especially of legumes and brassicas. These foods are not digestible by their young, called squabs, so adults overcome the problem by producing in their crop a curd-like substance of half-digested seed, called 'pigeon's milk'. Several species of pigeon and dove are found in the Peruvian Andes. The band-tailed pigeon (*Patagioenas fasciata*) occurs in large flocks in the cloud forest, while the bare-faced ground-dove (*Metriopelia ceciliae*) is often seen in small family groups on the red-tiled roofs of Andean towns. This latter species is called *casabellita* in Spanish, due to the whirring noise of its wings when taking off. Other species to look for include the

eared dove (*Zenaida auriculata*), plumbeous pigeon (*Columba plumbea*), spot-winged pigeon (*C. maculosa*), white-tipped dove (*Leptotila verreauxi*) and black-winged ground-dove (*Metriopelia melanoptera*).

HUMMINGBIRDS

The last of the non-passerine birds to warrant a mention are those glittering jewels of the Andes, the hummingbirds. Hummingbirds (family Trochilidae) are strictly American, having evolved in the Andes, and include some of the smallest birds in the world. They are uniquely adapted to extract nectar from flowers, possessing specially designed bills and tongues for the purpose, and many are important pollinators of flowers. Most hover to extract nectar, but some larger species perch when feeding. Hovering requires hummingbirds to beat their wings at 22–78 beats per second, which produces the characteristic humming sound from which they derive their name. Flexible shoulder joints permit a unique figure-of-eight stroke of each wing, which gives hummingbirds such control that, uniquely among birds, they can even fly backwards. Most hummingbirds have brightly coloured, iridescent plumage, some with ornate plumes on the head and extravagantly

Top Giant hummingbird (RW)
Above Marvellous spatuletail (HP)

modified tail feathers. In the Andes some species hover for insects as well as nectar. Because of the low temperatures, many, such as the olivaceous thornbill (*Chalcostigma olivaceum*) and the hillstars (*Oreotrochilus* spp.), become torpid at night in order to save energy.

Over 130 species of hummingbird are found in Peru, the majority of which occur in the Andes. They vary from the small metaltails (*Metallura* spp.), and the medium-sized sunangels (*Heliangelus* spp.) and pufflegs (*Eriocnemis* spp.), to the world's largest hummingbird, the giant hummingbird (*Patagonia gigas*), which measures up 23cm. This species is dull compared with many, but so large as to resemble Old World bee-eaters in flight. Among the most eye-catching species are those with long tail streamers, including the booted rackettail (*Ocreatus underwoodii*), the trainbearers (*Lesbia* spp.), the long-tailed sylph (*Aglaiocercus kingi*) and the Peruvian sheartail (*Thaumastura cora*). Most of these species can be found in the Andean cloud forests, and the sheartail in many hotel gardens in Lima and Arequipa. In fact, gardens with ornamental plants are a prime location for hummingbirds. The king of all Andean hummingbirds is the marvellous spatuletail (*Loddigesia mirabilis*), which is endemic to a small part of northern Peru. The male sports 15cm-long, bare-shafted tail feathers that cross each other at the tips, each ending in large purplish-black rackets. To see this bird you must make a special trip to the department of Amazonas in northern Peru, where it occurs above the town of Pedro Ruiz in the Utcubamba River valley.

The long-tailed sylph is found in cloud forests. This is a male. (HP)

PASSERINES
SUB-OSCINE PASSERINES

Sub-oscine passerines are distinguished from oscine passerines by a structural difference in their syrinx, or voice organs. This group of birds includes some of South America's most enigmatic and sought-after species. They pose some tricky identification challenges for birdwatchers, with many species very similar to each other. But each has a different voice and occupies its own distinct habitat niche.

Ovenbirds

Ovenbirds or Furnariids (Furnariidae) are a large and very diverse family, characterised by their dull plumage, loud chattering songs and largely secretive habits. They are insectivorous, and many have characteristic long and dishevelled tail feathers. Their popular name is derived from a number of species, known locally as horneros, which build conspicuous rounded mud nests that resemble the mud ovens commonly used for cooking throughout the region. Some, such as the streak-fronted thornbird (*Phacelladomus striaticeps*), build bulky stick structures.

In the Peruvian High Andes the most commonly encountered ovenbirds are the high grassland species that occur above the tree line. Hikers along the Inca Trail

Slender-billed miner

or in the Huascaran National Park may flush common and slender-billed miners (*Geositta cunicularia* and *tenirirostris*). These medium-sized brown and rufous birds get their name from excavating their nests in exposed earth banks, due to the local lack of trees. Similar species that also excavate their nests, but can be differentiated by their cocked tail and sharply decurved bill, are the earthcreepers (*Upucerthia* spp.)

Cinclodes are common birds around human habitation, llama corrals and streams. They resemble small brown thrushes with fine bills, and are fond of walking across the ground. The commonest of several species are the bar-winged and white-winged Cinclodes (*Cinclodes fuscus* and *atacamensis*). However, two rare species also occur. The first is the endemic white-bellied cinclodes (*Cinclodes palliatus*), perhaps the most striking ovenbird due to its large size and bright white underparts, which lives on high Andean peat bogs. You might spot this species on bogs next to the Central Highway just before Ticlio Pass, when travelling from Lima into the interior. The second is the royal cinclodes (*Cinclodes aricomae*). Once thought to be extinct, this species was rediscovered by the authors in the mid 1980s and has since been found to be surviving in isolated High Andean *Polylepis* woodland. Many trekking routes in the Cordillera Vilcanota pass through patches of *Polylepis*, particularly those at Mantanay, Yanacocha and Abra Malaga. Lucky trekkers might see one of these birds frantically 'moss-tossing' amongst the moss clumps on the ground and on rocky cliff faces. Another endangered ovenbird of *Polylepis* woodland is the white-browed tit-spinetail (*Letasthenura xenothorax*). This wonderfully patterned bird has a long slender tail, streaked back and rusty crown. It is easily found at Mantanay and Yanacocha, foraging acrobatically amongst the outermost branches.

Canasteros come in various similar-looking forms and can be tricky to tell apart. Some species inhabit pure bunchgrass (*Ichu*), some remnant forest fragments and others the interface between the two. Canastero is Spanish for 'basket', a reference to the basket-like nests these birds build close to the ground. The wren-like rushbird (*Phleocryptes melanops*) is an ovenbird that makes its home exclusively in the reedbeds of High Andean lakes, and can be found cheek by jowl with the spectacular flycatcher, the many-coloured rush-tyrant.

In the humid forests, one encounters more elusive and inconspicuous groups of ovenbirds that betray their presence only by their simple songs. A common sound is the repetitive note of the Azara's spinetail (*Synallaxis azarae*), named after Félix Manuel de Azara, a Spanish military officer and naturalist of the late 1700s, who also has many other creatures named after him. The pearled treerunner (*Magarornis squamiger*) is an attractive species of the forest understorey, which climbs tree trunks in the manner of a woodpecker and investigates the undersides of branches. Its underparts are plain brown, heavily spotted in a rich creamy yellow. The montane woodcreeper (*Lepidocolaptes lacrymiger*) is a common species of the higher elevation cloud forest that is often seen working its way along the main trunks of trees, usually in mixed feeding flocks with other birds.

Ground antbirds

Ground antbirds (*Formicariidae*) are dull-coloured species with cryptic camouflage plumage that mostly inhabit the mossy cloud forest understorey and are usually detected by their whistled calls. Antbirds do not eat ants; their name is derived from a handful of Amazonian species that habitually follow columns of army ants, snatching up insect prey that the marauding insects flush out – though no Andean species does this. There are two main kinds of ground antbird: anthrushes, which walk on the ground, and antpittas (named for their resemblance to Old World pittas), which hop along the ground or in low vegetation. In the early morning and late evening you might be lucky enough to spot one of these otherwise elusive birds hopping out onto a trail. Species that

Undulated antpitta

you may encounter in the Chachapoyas area include rusty-tinged antpitta (*Grallaria przewalskii*), chestnut antpitta (*Grallaria blakei*) and the rare, endemic pale-billed antpitta (*Grallaria carrikeri*). In the cloud forests of the Manu National Park and the Machu Picchu Historical Sanctuary an entirely different group of species can be found, including the endemic red-and-white antpitta (*Grallaria erythroleuca*), the rufous antpitta (*Grallaria rufa*) and the large undulated antpitta (*Grallaria squamigera*). The striking stripe-headed antpitta (*Grallaria andicola*) of central and southern Peru is one of the few antpitta species that ranges out into open ground to forage amongst grass tussocks and boulders.

Cotingas and cock-of-the-rock

Cotingas are only found in the American tropics. These arboreal species vary greatly in size, and many species make their home in the High Andes – some of them with quite a strange appearance. The word 'cotinga' is derived from the native name for an Amazonian species, the white bellbird (*Procnias alba*), and means 'whitewashed'. Despite this, cotingas are best known for their bright colours, especially in the males. They use this showy plumage to impress females, often at organised gatherings, known as leks.

Among the cotinga family is the spectacular Andean cock-of-the-rock (*Rupicola peruviana*), which you might be lucky enough to see in the upper reaches of the cloud forest, beneath Machu Picchu or along the road to Manu. As if sporting bright red plumage and a bizarre crest weren't enough, each male also has to perform his courtship dance for females in front of an assembled crowd of other males – and often tourists! Other species are less showy. Those you might encounter in the cloud forest include the red-crested cotinga (*Ampelion rubrochristatus*), which is fairly common along the Inca Trail to Machu Picchu, the chestnut-crested cotinga (*Ampelion rufaxilla*) and the white-cheeked cotinga (*Zaratornis stresemanni*). This last species, a Peruvian endemic, is best looked for feeding on the reddish-orange berries of *Tristerix* mistletoes that decorate the *Polylepis* woodlands of the Huascaran National Park – in particular around Llanganuco Lakes.

Fruiteaters are among the most stunning members of the cotinga group, and specialise in feeding on fruiting *melastome* bushes and trees. The endemic masked fruiteater (*Pipreola pulchra*) can be regularly found in the cloud forests around Machu Picchu, or in the Cordillera Carpish in central Peru.

Other sub-oscines

The tapaculos (*Scytalopus* spp.) are extremely secretive, small grey birds of forest and timberline that you are unlikely to see without careful searching. Furthermore, they all look the same and can be regularly identified in the field by only their songs or biochemical anlysis of blood or tissue samples. Tyrant-flycatchers have radiated into every possible Neotropical habitat, from the windswept puna grasslands to the lush cloud forests and everything in between. They vary in shape and size, and the sexes are usually similar in appearence. They are also tricky to identify for the most part, and comprise many smaller groups such as kingbirds, pygmy-tyrants, flycatchers, tyrants, tyrannulets, tody-flycatchers, tody-tyrants, elaenias, pewees, becards and phoebes – to name just a few.

Cinnamon flycatchers are often found in pairs in the cloud forest.

Andean cock-of-the-rock (male) (PP)

CULTIVATION AND BIRD CONSERVATION

It is no coincidence that areas rich in endemic birds are often close to historical centres of culture, such as Machu Picchu. This is because the local environmental and climatic conditions suit both birds and people. Machu Picchu lies at the junction of the humid low Urubamba basin and the benign Vilcanota Valley that was the 'breadbasket' of Inca culture. Some of the rarest Andean birds are thus found in forest fragments that surround the more isolated Inca ruins and terraces of the area.

Habitat disturbance in these areas is nothing new: evidence from lake sediments suggests that the Machu Picchu area was totally deforested and degraded some 1,000–4,000 years ago. The Incas, however, subsequently introduced sustainable agro-forestry systems. This, combined with a climatic warming period from about 1100AD, encouraged the return of the forests. But with the arrival of the Spanish in the 1530s, land management practices changed and the forests became increasingly overexploited. This has continued until today, and sadly many species in the Andes are now on the verge of extinction.

A major challenge for conservation biologists is now how to conserve biodiversity in areas close to dense rural populations. Andean cloud forest is unsuited to intensive agriculture: its shallow topsoil washes away, once exposed, and fields must be left fallow for long periods. But new roads have allowed larger areas to be opened up and today much of the Cusco area is severely degraded. Highlands are routinely burned to stop forest encroachment and provide pasture – and even from a local belief that the smoke can help bring rain. Today the treeline is located several 100m below its natural position. Perhaps only 1% of *Polylepis* forest remains, and this is fragmented into isolated patches where some of the world's rarest birds still survive.

Conservation needs are often in conflict with poverty-driven pressures on the natural environment. Striking a balance between the needs of people and wildlife can be difficult in countries such as Peru, where socio-economic problems inevitably take priority. Positive strategies include creating a network of reserves, and improving land use, with education as the essential ingredient. However, the distribution of birds causes further problems. Conservationists have traditionally focused on areas with the most species, which are often sparsely populated regions with little conflict of interest. But this is not necessarily the best way to reduce extinction rates, since it leaves many of the rarest and most localised species unprotected. Studies at London's Natural History Museum have shown that a minimum set of 28 target areas are needed to protect all Peruvian birds. Each has its own particular specialities. Machu Picchu, for instance, contains six threatened species that are not covered in any other of the 28 target areas: royal cinclodes, white-browed tit-spinetail, Junín canastero (*Asthenes virgata*), Inca wren (*Thryothorus eisenmanni*), cusco brush-finch (*Atlapetes canicep*) and Parodi's hemispingus (*Hemispingus parodi*).

OSCINE PASSERINES

A very large number of oscine passerine species (the true 'songbirds') have been recorded in the Peruvian High Andes. So many, that there is only room here to discuss briefly a few species you are most likely to encounter. Many, though by no means all, are typical 'small brown jobs' – especially the cryptically coloured females.

Swallows (Hirundidae)

Swallows are familiar to many as harbingers of spring, and are quite at home perched on telephone wires. They are not quite as agile in the air as the superficially similar but unrelated swifts (Apodidae), but are more graceful, using their forked tails to bank and pitch in pursuit of flying insects. Swallows also tend to fly closer to the ground than swifts, meaning that the two types of bird avoid competing for the same food supply. The common High Andean species is the brown-bellied swallow (*Notiochelidon murina*), often seen in town squares and nesting in churches. The Andean swallow (*Petrochelidon andecola*) is somewhat less common and likely to be seen on only the highest grasslands, often along streams. The blue-and-white swallow (*Notiochelidon cyanoleuca*) is found at slightly lower elevations, and nests inside the crevices in the ancient terracing at Machu Picchu.

Thrushes

Another family recognisable to most is the thrushes (Turdidae), and several species are found in the highlands. The common 'garden' thrush of the inter-montane valleys is the chiguanco thrush (*Turdus chiguanco*), whose name is an anglicisation of its native Quechua name *chihuanco*. This large brown thrush somewhat resembles a female European blackbird (*Turdus merula*) and has a similar liquid song. It is replaced in the moist cloud forest by the great thrush (*Turdus fuscater*), which is larger and blacker. An atypical thrush, with an unmistakable, piercingly rhythmic song, is the Andean solitaire (*Myadestes ralloides*), which is common along the river below Machu Picchu. It is slate-grey below, warm brown above and has white outer tail feathers.

Female Chighuanco thrush (HP)

Wrens and dippers

The song of the house wren (*Troglodytes aedon*) is a familiar sound to visitors from North America. In the mossy cloud forests and especially in bamboo patches, some larger members of the wren family (Troglodytidae) also occur. These are all great singers, and both males and females combine in exquisite duets, generally regarded as being among the best birdsongs of the region. In northern and central Peru, you may find Sharpe's wren (*Cinnycerthia olivascens*), Peruvian wren (*Cinnycerthia peruana*) and plain-tailed wren (*Thrylothorus euophrys*). In southern Peru, the Inca Wren (*Thryloythorus eisenmanni*) has only recently been formally described to science, after being discovered not far from Machu Picchu – from where it is easily found. A close relative of the wrens is the white-capped dipper (*Cinclus leucocephalus*), which is a

White-capped dipper

common sight on rushing Andean streams and rivers. Dippers are the only passerines that habitually duck beneath the water's surface to find their food. They are easily seen along the Rio Urubamba from the tourist train to Machu Picchu.

Tanagers

The tanagers (Thraupinae) comprise a large and varied family that contains some of the most strikingly coloured birds of the Peruvian Andes. They can be broken down into distinctive sub-groups, including tanagers, euphonias, hemispinguses, chlorophonias, flowerpiercers, conebills, honeycreepers and dacnises. At least 60 species are known from the Machu Picchu area and 90 in Manu. Tanagers are generalist in their feeding habits, taking a variety of foods including caterpillars, seeds and berries. Some are rather finch-like, while others resemble thrushes. Flowerpiercers have specially adapted hooked and upturned bills used for piercing the base of flowers to get at their nectar, thus cheating the hummingbirds that share their forest edges and shrubby habitats. Conebills are small, warbler-like tanagers with pointed bills. Bush-tanagers roam in family groups and stick to the mid-and under-storey of cloud forests. Hemispinguses often like bamboo and are strictly Andean. The true tanagers are found in mixed fruit-eating flocks in the canopy and sub-canopy of the cloud forest.

Seed eaters

A range of seed-eating passerines, including grosbeaks, saltators and finches, are found in the Andes, and many are highly conspicuous. Brush-finches typically inhabit the edges of cloud forests, whilst seedeaters are often nomadic, wandering over vast distances, with female-plumaged birds greatly outnumbering male-plumaged birds in any one flock. Sierra-finches are a common inhabitant of the more open grasslands and inter-montane valleys, particularly around farmland. Common species in the Cusco area include golden-billed saltator (*Saltator aurantiirostris*), black-backed grosbeak (*Pheucticus aureoventris*), band-tailed seedeater (*Catamenia analis*), greenish-yellow finch (*Sicalis olivascens*), Peruvian sierra-finch (*Phrygilus punensis*) and hooded siskin (*Carduelis magellanica*).

Blackbirds

New World blackbirds (Icterinae) are scarce in the Andes, but with a little effort, you may be able to find two or three species. The yellow-winged blackbird (*Agelaius thilus*) is common in the south around reed-fringed lakes such as Lake Titicaca. Both the southern mountain cacique (*Cacicus chrysonotus*) and yellow-billed cacique (*Amblycercus holosericeus*) inhabit the cloud forest on the humid eastern slopes. The former hangs around in small flocks of up to six individuals and often reveals itself by its quavering, melodic song, whilst the latter is slightly more secretive, preferring dense *Chusquea* bamboo patches.

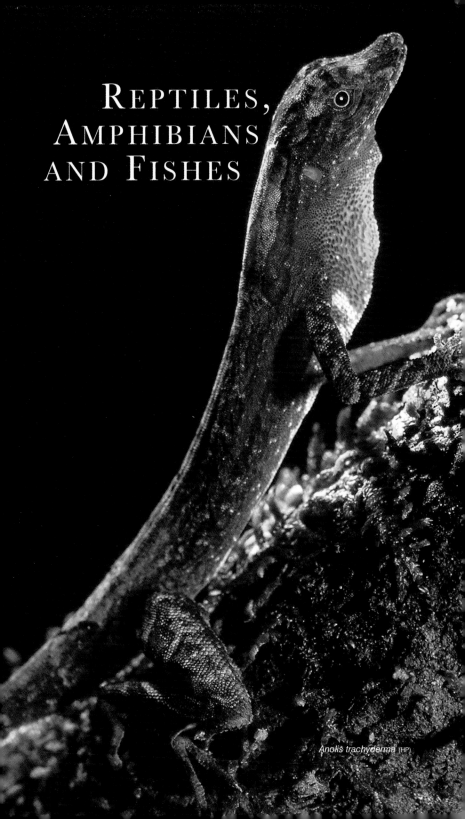

REPTILES, AMPHIBIANS AND FISHES

Anolis trachyderma (HP)

REPTILES

Reptiles are described as 'cold-blooded' or, in more scientific terms, ectothermic. This means they do not generate enough heat to maintain a constant body temperature, so must gain or lose heat from their immediate environment. It also means that they can survive on much less food than most mammals and birds, which burn up most of their food in creating and maintaining body heat. Almost all reptiles are covered in scales, and the majority of species are egg-laying (oviparous).

Reptiles in the Peruvian Andes are restricted to lizards and snakes (order Squamata), and these are found in almost every possible niche. Many are difficult to identify, and herpetologists can often only do so by catching them and taking detailed measurements. However, it is best to avoid handling reptiles and stick to simply observing them. Many Andean lizards are relatively fearless and, with patience, will allow you to approach closely. Snakes, on the other hand, should never be handled, except under the strict supervision of a specialised guide.

LIZARDS

Most lizards are immediately distinguished from snakes by having legs. Unlike snakes, they also possess eyelids and so are able to blink. A translucent inner, or third eyelid called the 'nictitating membrane' can be drawn across their eyes to protect them from damage. Snake eyelids, by contrast, become fused when they are still embryos, so that they develop as transparent protective scales called spectacles that are generally shed when the snake moults its skin. Lizards also have a prehensile tongue used for feeding, whereas snake tongues have evolved into sensory organs used solely for 'tasting' the air. Furthermore, no lizard (with the exception of two species from North America) has a venomous bite, and lizards cannot dislocate their jaws, as snakes can, for the purpose of swallowing food, so generally feed on smaller

One of several species of spectacled lizard (HP)

food items. Finally, lizards are able to drop their tails as a defence mechanism when captured or threatened, with a new tail regenerating over a period of time. This ability, known as autotomy (literally 'self-cutting'), is painless, but it is a further reminder of why Andean lizards should not be handled.

As a rule, the numbers of species in all reptile genera in the Peruvian Andes increases with descending elevation, as conditions become warmer and habitats more congenial. Few species are adapted to survive the cold conditions of the higher Andean habitats. Those that are tend to be dark in colour, enabling them to absorb solar radiation and warm up more quickly. These include the Gymnophthalmids, meaning 'naked-eyed'. These small, secretive and largely diurnal lizards reach their highest levels of diversity in the Peruvian Andes. They have elongated bodies (up to about 10cm) and relatively short limbs. Most have transparent 'windows' in their lower eyelids, allowing them to see even when their eyes are 'closed'.

Spectacled lizards

Spectacled lizards (*Proctoporus* spp.) are more elongate and thin-bodied when compared to other Andean lizard species. These small (10 cm length) darkly coloured lizards are generally found at 2,600-4,100m in the departments of Junín, Ayacucho, Apurimac, Cusco and Puno. Recently, what was long thought to be a single species, the commonly encountered Andean Spectacled Lizard (*Proctoporus bolivianus*), was found to comprise three species, the other two being the Apurimac Spectacled Lizard (*Proctoporus sucullucu*) and Cusco Spectacled Lizard (*Proctoporus unsaacae*). Each inhabits a slightly different geographic area throughout the cordilleras of southern Peru and northern Bolivia. New species of spectacled lizard continue to be discovered throughout the Peruvian Andes, most recently the Apolobamba Spectacled Lizard (*Proctoporus subsolanus*), which can be found by carefully turning over rocks, often in places with agricultural terracing, near Sandia, Puno. Eighty-nine percent of all known spectacled-lizard species occur in the Andes, making up 2.3% of the total Andean lizard fauna.

Other small lizards

Closely related to spectacled lizards are the *Euspondylus* and *Alopoglossus* forest lizards. These can often be found moving in and out of small crevices in banks of leaf litter along cloud forest streams and low-lying areas. They resemble skinks, with smooth scales and reduced limbs, and feed primarily on insects and other invertebrates. Newly discovered species of both *Euspondylus* (green body interspersed with bluish patches) and *Alopoglossus* lizards (brown body, becoming blacker towards the tail) have recently been found in the Megantoni National Sanctuary, in the Cordillera Vilcabamba.

The *Prionodactylus* naked-eyed lizards are streamlined arboreal species living on woody shrubs and vines. Species such as *Prionodactylus manicatus* can be found in the Megantoni National Reserve and the Cordillera Azul National Park, of southern and central Peru respectively, foraging at the base of trees or around fallen logs, or sleeping in tree hollows in the cloud forests. The *Neusticurus* stream-lizards, also

Leaf-iguanas can appear quite intimidating but are perfectly harmless. (HP)

belonging to the Gymnophthalmidae family, are semi-aquatic and commonly found at the cloud forest–stream interface. The varying depth of cloud forest leaf litter also provides a suitable microhabitat in which to find tiny, dark-coloured *Iphisa* lizards. The minute limbless worm-lizards (genus *Bachia*) are among the most bizarre lizards of the Peruvian Andes. Their vestigial limbs serve as tiny paddles for pushing and pulling themselves through the leaf litter or around rotting logs in search of their favourite food, termites.

Leaf-iguanas

Leaf-iguanas (*Stenocercus* spp.) are fairly common in arid montane scrub habitats dominated by agave plants and cacti. These lizards belong to the Iguanidae family, one of the most species-rich groups of reptiles in South America, and are slender, small-to-medium in size and often cryptically coloured. A number of different species occur in the upper valleys at 1,500–3,900m in the Rio Perene region of the central Peruvian Andes. They include variable leaf-iguana (*Stenocercus variabilis*), Boettger's leaf-iguana (*Stenocercus boettgeri*) and ornate leaf-iguana (*Stenocercus praeornatus*). The newly described Mantaro leaf-iguana (*Stenocercus frittsi*) can only be found in the upper valleys of the Rio Mantaro drainage in the departments of Huancavelica and Ayacucho, at elevations of 2,300–4,000m.

Geckos

Geckos (Gekkonidae family) have bead-like scales that give them a rubbery appearance. These small lizards are famed for their ability to cling to walls and ceilings with their specially adapted toes. The Peruvian Andes are home to a number of endemic species belonging to the genus *Pseudogonatodes*, or clawed geckos. These tiny lizards are dark in colour with reddish underparts, and spend most of their time climbing around small plants and tree trunks, tirelessly searching for invertebrate prey. The Peruvian clawed gecko (*Pseudogonatodes peruvianus*) can be found in the remnant cloud forest patches of the Rio Utcubamba Valley, while Barbour's clawed gecko (*Pseudogonatodes barbouri*) is a common inhabitant of the inter-Andean valleys of northwestern Peru.

Anoles

Another common lizard group of the Peruvian cloud forests is the anoles (Polychrotidae), an insectivorous and largely arboreal family, whose slender bodies and highly elongated tails reach a total length of 8–18 cm. Several species are able to change their colour, and most are highly agile, running effortlessly up and down walls and tree trunks. Males display by bobbing their heads, while extending and retracting their colourful dewlap to intimidate rivals. Little is known about the taxonomy and ecology of anoles in the Peruvian Andes, and ongoing studies aim to determine the number of species and their geographic distributions. Two common species are the slender anole (*Anolis fuscoauratus*) and bark anole (*Anolis ortonii*).

SNAKES

Snakes are legless reptiles, closely related to lizards. All species are carnivorous, eating prey such as small mammals, birds, eggs and even insects. Most are fairly secretive and nocturnal, which makes it difficult to observe them. Furthermore, the majority of species that occur in the Peruvian Andes do not have common names and it can be tricky to learn their scientific names.

Non-venomous snakes

Most snakes found in the Andes are non-venomous. The species you are most likely to encounter are the whipsnakes, or racers (*Chironius* spp.). These harmless, slender green snakes, most of which have yellowish undersides, can measure 1m or more. One species, the sipos snake (*Chironius monticola*), is found in the cloud forests of Amazonas, Cajamarca and San Martin in northern Peru; Huanuco and Junín in central Peru; and Cusco and Puno in southern Peru at 1,500–2,500m.

Blunt-headed tree snake (*Imantodes cenchoa*) (HP)

Other common cloud forest species include the beautiful little frog-eating snake (*Leimadophis reginae*), with its bright yellow and black markings, the arboreal blunt-headed tree snake (*Imantodes cenchoa*), the marcapata false coral snake (*Oxyrhopus marcapatae*), which is endemic to the Urubamba and Marcapata valleys in southern Peru, and the short-nosed ground snake (*Taeniophallus brevirostris*). A new Taeniophallus species, with a black body, white rings and pink dorsal blotches, has recently been discovered in the Santuario Nacional Megantoni, in southern Peru.

When exploring the *Polylepis* woodlands of Mantanay, Yanacocha in the Cordillera Vilcanota, or around the Llanganuco glacial lakes in the Huascaran National Park, at 3,000m or above, you may come across the Peruvian slender snake (*Tachymenis peruviana*) as it patrols the tree branches for prey. Known as a 'false viper', or 'viper mimic', this darkly patterned snake is one of the few species that can cope with the extreme climate of these environments. Other high altitude slender snakes include *Tachymenis affinis*, found only in the department of Huanuco; *Tachymenis elongata* of Ancash and Piura; and *Tachymenis tarmensis*, found in the high forests of the department of Junín.

Venomous snakes

Two groups of venomous snakes are represented in the cloud and elfin forests of the Peruvian Andes: the Elapids (coral snakes) and the Viperids (lanceheads and vipers). These snakes are not easy to see and you should consider yourself lucky if you find one. However, do not approach too close or disturb it: snake bites can be fatal!

Coral snakes (*Micrurus* spp.) belong to the Elapidae group. They earn their name from their pattern of contrasting colour bands, making them reminiscent of coral-bead necklaces. These secretive snakes spend most of their time buried in the ground or in leaf litter. Their single pair of very small fangs is positioned at the front of their top jaw, to deliver venom. However, coral snakes are mild mannered and not prone to biting.

SNAKES, BEWARE THE MUSSARANA!

Mussarana

One of the most common cloud forest species (also found in the tropical lowlands) is the smooth, glossy mussarana (*Clelia clelia*). This diurnal species is non-venomous to humans and can reach 2m in length. It is a light pink-reddish colour when young, becoming lead-blue/black as it matures. The mussarana has a remarkable ability to prey upon other snakes, including vipers. It has 10–15 strong teeth positioned at the back of its mouth, which it uses to grasp the head of its victim and then to work it into its gullet. It then coils its body around its prey and kills it by constriction, before finally consuming it whole. The mussarana is immune to the venom of the snakes it feeds on. In some regions of Latin America farmers keep these snakes as pets in order to reduce the number of vipers on their farms!

The Inca forest pit viper is well camouflaged. (DD/A)

They also have relatively small mouths and much smaller fangs than vipers, and some species have difficulty penetrating thick clothing or hiking boots. It is rare to see coral snakes in the Peruvian Andes; they are much more diverse and more easily found in the tropical lowland forests. However, lucky visitors may come across one of the more common lower elevation cloud forest species, the Andean black-backed coral snake (*Leptomicrurus narducci*).

Vipers (Viperidae) are typically rather stocky snakes with arrowhead-shaped heads and overlapping scales. A number of species occur in the Peruvian Andes, the most widespread being the Andean lancehead (*Bothrops andianus*). This small to medium-sized dark grey viper has dark triangular or diamond-shaped markings along its upper body. The brightly coloured and intricately patterned Inca forest pit viper (*Bothriopsis oligolepis*) has a more restricted range and is only found only at a handful of sites in the central and southern Peruvian cordilleras. The fairly dull-coloured Peruvian pit viper (*Bothriopsis peruviana*) is found in the extreme southern Andes or Peru.

AMPHIBIANS

Amphibians are cold-blooded animals that are adapted to aquatic environments, although many species spend most of their time on land. Unlike reptiles, they have smooth sensitive skin through which they are able to breath. Most species depend on fresh water for reproduction.

FROGS AND TOADS

Frogs and toads belong to the order *Anura*, which means 'without tails', referring to the fact that these animals lose their tails as they develop into adults. There are a few diagnostic differences between the two, but generally speaking, frogs have wet, smooth skin and tend to leap, while toads have dryer, warty skin and tend to 'walk'. Frogs also generally lay their eggs in clusters, whereas – with some exceptions – toads lay theirs in long chains. Toads also have parotoid glands, which show as a lump behind each eye, that secrete toxins when they are threatened.

The frogs of the Peruvian Andes exhibit a great variety of form and behaviour. They are not the easiest of wildlife to see, being generally small and camouflaged, and often nocturnal. However, with a little patience and a good flashlight, you might find that searching carefully through the leaf litter and along the edges of ponds and streams proves very fruitful. Remember that frogs and toads breathe through their skin and are very sensitive to anything they come into contact with. Furthermore, some species secrete chemicals that act as irritants. So it is best to avoid handling amphibians.

Frog diversity in the Peruvian Andes reaches its peak in the humid cloud forest habitats. The number of species gradually decreases with increasing elevation. However, even in the high altiplano habitats, including lakes at 5,200–5,400m, you can still find a number of specially adapted species. These include *Pleurodema* foam-nesting frogs and *Telmatobius* water frogs, which are strictly aquatic and often endemic to specific lakes. Some species, such as the Lake Titicaca water-frog (*Telmatobius coleus*), are very large, with loose, wrinkled skin that enables them to absorb more oxygen from the water. This also enables them to remain submerged for long periods, so protecting themselves from higher levels of ultraviolet radiation and also various daytime predators.

ANDEAN FROGS

Members of the genus *Phrynopus*, often referred to as Andean frogs, are among the most bizarre creatures of the Peruvian Andes. More than 20 different *Phrynopus* species are found in Peru, and all of them lack ears – either external or internal. This unusual deficiency has been reported for several other species, particularly from the central Peruvian Andes. How these frogs communicate or hear remains a complete mystery.

Water frogs (*Telmatobius* sp.) are strictly aquatic. (TM/SAP)

THE ENDEMIC FROGS OF LAKE JUNÍN

Lake Junín is a permanent, but fairly shallow freshwater lake located at 4,082m in the high altiplano of central Peru. Known as *Chinchaycocha* in Quechua, it is the second largest lake in Peru, and home to numerous endemic flora and fauna. The area has been officially designated as the Junín National Reserve and as a wetlands site of international importance. It covers an area of 53,000ha, of which almost 40,000 comprise the lake and associated marshes. However, despite this protection, the lake's unique wildlife includes some of the most threatened species in Peru – in particular its endemic amphibians. These were once common and widespread throughout the lake, but species such as the Lake Junín giant frog (*Batrachophrynus macrostomus*) and the Junín Andean frog (*Phrynopus juninensis*), both of which are exclusively aquatic, have undergone dramatic population declines over the last 20 years. At the outflow of Lake Junín, at the Rio Upamayo, a hydro-electric power station influences the water level, causing adverse fluctuations during drought years that have serious consequences for the frog populations. The inflow of mining residues, coupled with the sewage from the cities of Junín and Carhuamayo, has increased water pollution levels, while the predation of eggs and tadpoles by introduced rainbow trout and uncontrolled local exploitation as a food source have also contributed to the frogs' decline. Measures are urgently required to control all levels of harvesting, water-level regulation and pollution in order to save these unique creatures from extinction.

Robber-frogs

Montane species of the genus *Eleutherodactylus*, sometimes called robber-frogs, are among the most difficult Andean frogs to identify by sight. They are cryptically coloured and common inhabitants of the cloud forest, where they can be either terrestrial or arboreal. All species are characterised by having direct development, in which the offspring hatch from eggs as miniature versions of adults ('froglets'), thus bypassing the tadpole stage. Many also display parental care: either the males or females will guard the eggs once they have been laid – and sometimes even the froglets after hatching. Scientists have suggested that this may explain the evolutionary and ecological success of the genus. Terrestrial robber-frogs, such as *Eleutherodactylus fenestratus*, can often be found during the day beside cloud forest streams, where they normally hunt for flies. Other species, such as the manakin robber-frog (*Eleutherodactylus salaputium*) and long-legged robber-frog (*Eleutherodactylus cruralis*) can be found by sifting through the leaf litter underfoot.

Marsupial tree frogs

Among the largest and most common frogs of the cloud forest are the marsupial tree frogs (*Gastrotheca* spp.), which derive their name from the brood pouch on the female's back. During reproduction, the male first fertilises the eggs on her lower back, and then inserts them into this brood pouch using his toes. The eggs remain in contact with the female's vascular tissue throughout, which provides them with oxygen. Several marsupial tree frog species have highly distinct casqued skulls – an adaptation related to protection and shelter within the tree canopy. One of the most striking Peruvian species is the helmeted marsupial frog (*Gastrotheca galeata*), found only in the western slope montane forest habitats around Canchaque, at 1,740–2,130m, on the Cordillera de Huancabamba. It is unusual amongst this group for being terrestrial. The Cusco marsupial frog (*Gastrotheca ochoai*) is a common species of the Cordillera Vilcanota cloud forests, at around 2,700m. New species of this group continue to be discovered in Peru.

Common tree frogs

Closely related to marsupial tree frogs are the Hylids (family Hylidae), also known as common tree frogs. These are rarely dominant among cloud forest frogs, with only six species known from the Peruvian Andes. They are mainly arboreal, insectivorous and are generally green in colour – although some terrestrial and aquatic hylids are brown. Ochoa's bromeliad frog (*Hyla antoniiochoai*) is found only in the higher elevation cloud forests at Esperanza, along the Manu road (below the Acjanacu guard station of Manu National Park). Only described in 2005, this secretive species appears to be dependent on arboreal bromeliads.

Poison frogs

Poison frogs (Dendrobatidae family), often referred to as poison-dart frogs, are typically small and black with brightly coloured patterns that warn predators of their alkaloid toxins. Most species are terrestrial, and often sit with an erect posture on the forest floor. Their common name alludes to the use of their skins by indigenous South American people for the manufacture of poisons that are applied to arrows or blow-gun darts. Poison frogs are less well represented in the Peruvian Andes than in the lower rainforests. Silverstone's poison frog (*Epipedobates silverstonei*) is a colourful terrestrial species found in the lower cloud forest habitats of Cordillera Azul National Park. Sira poison frog (*Dendrobates sirensis*) is a highly mobile, arboreal species restricted to the Cerros de Sira, an isolated mountain range in the same region. The *Colostethus* genus of poison frogs is unlike any other in this family. These species are not usually brightly coloured or poisonous. Females lay their eggs on the ground following a quite elaborate courtship display by the male. One parent (generally the male) guards the eggs until they hatch. The newly hatched tadpoles then wriggle onto the back of either the male or female parent, who transports them to water.

Glass frogs

Glass frogs (Centrolenidae family) are arboreal frogs most often found along montane forest streams and rivers, which reach their highest

Silverstone's poison dart frog

diversity in Peru's cloud forests. They are generally green, but the underside of some species is transparent. This means that not only do they blend in with their backgrounds very effectively, but also their internal structure is partially visible. Glass frogs are often confused with robber-frogs, but can easily be distinguished by their forward-facing eyes (those of robber-frogs face outwards). They also have very specific methods of laying their eggs on leaves that overhang montane streams and small rivers. In many species, once the eggs are deposited, the parents fend off parasitic flies that try to lay their own eggs on those of the frogs. The tadpoles, with their powerful tails, are well adapted to life in fast-flowing montane streams. The Cuzco cochran frog (*Cochranella spiculata*), Berger's glass frog (*Hyalinobatrachium bergeri*) and emerald glass frog (*Centrolene prosoblepon*) are all found along the road to Manu National Park.

Toads

One of the most threatened toad species (family Bufonidae) of the Peruvian Andes is the Peruvian stubfoot toad (*Atelopus peruensis*). This species is now listed as critically endangered, with its population having undergone an estimated 80% decline in the last ten years – probably caused by *chytridiomycosis* (see *Fungi and Lichen*, page 49). The veragua toad (*Bufo veraguensis*) is one of the more common Andean toads, being found in the cloud forests of the Marcapata Valley (near Cuzco)

and the Ayacucho region. The carabaya stubfoot toad (*Atelopus erythropus*) is endemic to the southern Peruvian Cordilleras.

SALAMANDERS AND CAECILIANS
Salamanders

Salamanders are extremely rare in the Peruvian Andes. These amphibians resemble small lizards, but differ from them in lacking scales. Normally terrestrial and dark-coloured, they typically have very slender bodies, short

The endangered Peruvian stubfoot toad (HP)

legs, long tails and moist skin, and are famous for their capacity to regenerate lost limbs. Peruvian species belong to the genus *Bolitoglossa*, which means 'projectile tongue' – a reference to how they capture their prey. The intriguingly named Peruvian mushroom-tongue salamander (*Bolitoglossa peruviana*) has a fairly wide distribution throughout the Peruvian Andes. Found in the lower montane forests of Moyobamba, in northern Peru, this species seems able to tolerate habitat modification. The Rio Santa Rosa salamander (*Bolitoglossa digitigrada*) is known only from the Rio Santa Rosa area, in Ayacucho.

Caecilians

Caecilians are strange, limbless, worm-like amphibians that can reach over a metre in length. They live in the soft, moist humus of the forest floor and, as a result, are among the least-known amphibians of the Peruvian Andes. All caecilians have lungs, and breathe oxygen through their mouths and their extremely smooth skin. They have greatly reduced eyes, resulting in limited vision (in fact the name 'caecilian' is derived from the Latin *caecus*, meaning 'blind'). Caecilians also have two tentacles positioned on the head, which probably aid their sense of smell. It is very difficult to find caecilians in their natural habitat, but your best chance is early in the morning after heavy rains. One species is the Marcapata Valley caecilian (*Epicrionops peruvianus*), which is endemic to southeastern Peru.

FISHES

Although you are unlikely to see them very clearly, except perhaps in the nets of local fishermen, a great many fish species live in the lakes, marshes, streams, rivers and other watercourses of the Peruvian Andes. Our knowledge of their ecology and distribution is very limited.

CHARACIFORMS

The tetras and characins, sometimes known as the Characiforms, comprise the largest and best-known group of Andean fish. They are typically small to medium-sized, with lustrous flashes of metallic colours on their sides. These flashes are an adaptation to living in streams and rivers, where the waters are often murky and visibility is poor, and enable the fish to communicate with and identify one another using reflected light. Characiforms are principally omnivorous, although some have specialised vegetarian or carnivorous diets. Species such as *Astynax bimaculatus* and *Creagrutus changae* can be found in the lower elevation streams and smaller rivers of the eastern Andes.

CATFISH

The second most common group of fish is the Siluriforms, or catfish, so called because they use whisker-like filaments, or barbels, around their mouths to sense and locate items of food in the murky depths. Catfish are generally bottom feeders, consuming the detritus that sinks from above. *Trichomycterus* catfish (family Trichomycteridae) are usually found in the headwater streams of larger Andean lakes. These nocturnal fish have elongated bodies and are typically parasitic, attacking the gill tissue of much larger fishes. *Chaetostoma* catfish (Loricariidae) are common inhabitants of cloud forest streams at 1,700m–2,200m.

Among the most remarkable Andean fish are the naked sucker-mouth catfish (family *Astroblepidae*), the term 'naked' referring to their lack of scales. These fish have a number of unique adaptations for life in the fast-flowing waters of the Peruvian Andes, including an adhesive ventral mouth, hooks on their pelvic and pectoral fins, and a unique abdominal musculature that enables them to cling to steep, turbulent environments – including underwater cliff faces.

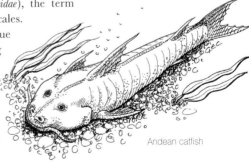
Andean catfish

FRESH FISH FOR THE INCA

Before the introduction of trout and kingfish to the Andes, there were no large species of fish to be caught for the Incas' dinner table. However, there was a solution. The Incas used a sophisticated system of roads and fast relay runners, called *Chaskis*, to courier fresh fish up from the coast in double-quick time. Only now is the ancient Inca Port (aptly named today Puerto Inca) being credited with the historical importance of having provided the nobility of Inca Cusco with fresh fish. Look on the map and you will see that Puerto Inca is the shortest distance from the seashore to Cusco.

KILLIFISH

Killifish are small fish with black-striped or barred bodies, usually 2.5–5cm in length, that belong to a group called Cyprinodonts (family Cyprinodontidae). The name is derived from the Dutch word *kilde*, meaning 'small creek' or 'puddle'. Many killifish are endemic to specific Andean lakes. Lake Titicaca has at least two species, *Orestias ispi* and *Orestias mulleri*. In central Peru, killifish endemic to Lake Junín form up to 80–90% of the diet of the critically endangered Junín flightless grebe (*Podiceps taczanowskii*).

Populations of many endemic species, such as the Titicaca killifish, are now under considerable threat. In 1939 trout were introduced into Lake Titicaca, as well as other lakes and rivers, as part of an aid scheme to provide protein-rich fish for local consumption. In those days the environmental impacts of introducing exotic species were not fully understood, and since then populations of native fish species have declined dramatically. Rainbow trout (*Oncorhynchus mykiss*) and other notable commercial introductions, such as the pejerrey, or kingfish (*Odontesthes bonariensis*), have flourished in their new homes by preying upon and outcompeting native fish, displacing many and even driving some to extinction. Very few watersheds now remain unaffected by human influence – one exception being those of the newly created Megantoni National Reserve, in the central part of the Urubamba Valley, where recent studies have discovered a new species of catfish.

MYSTERY SEAHORSE

The mystery of the fabled Lake Titicaca seahorse (*Hippocampus titicacaensis*) has long captivated fish enthusiasts. The Bolivian-German archaeologist Arthur Posnansky (1873–1946) named the species, having been given a dried specimen by a local Titicaca fisherman. He believed it to be the proof he had been seeking to show that the lake was once a sea that had since been raised up geologically along with the Andes. It was a contentious theory, given that Titicaca is a freshwater lake and contains no evidence of ever having been a marine habitat. The seahorse has not been seen since and it now seems highly likely that the specimen (now an exhibit in the Museum of Archaeology in Tiwanaku, Bolivia) actually originated from the Peruvian coast, perhaps intended as a tourist souvenir. The mystery is further compounded, however, by the existence of a 2,000-year-old ceramic seahorse, held in the same museum, which was unearthed in the Titicaca area. Desiccated seahorses are often to be found today in Andean markets, where medicinal herbs and magical charms are to be bought for use by *curandreros* (traditional healers).

INVERTEBRATES

Peruvian apple snail (HP)

The Peruvian Andes are still something of an unknown quantity in terms of their invertebrate biodiversity. To describe thoroughly even one particular group would require a lifetime's work. Inevitably perhaps, some have enjoyed more attention than others because they are seen as more interesting and attractive, or are simply easier to study. Many soft-bodied invertebrates occur in the Peruvian Andes, including earthworms (Annelida), freshwater clams and mussels (Bivalvia) and land snails (Gastropoda). But the groups that have been best studied, and are most likely to catch the attention of the visitor, belong to the order Arthropoda.

Arthropods (which means 'joint-footed'), are hard-bodied invertebrates that possess exoskeletons made from the polysaccharide chitin. They include the prodigious insects (Insecta), as well as arachnids (Arachnea), centipedes (Chilopoda), millipedes (Diplopoda) and woodlice (Isopoda).

Peruvian mountain centipede (HP)

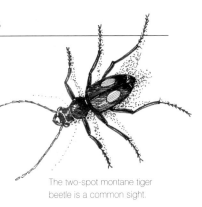

The two-spot montane tiger beetle is a common sight.

INSECTS

Insects are distinguished from other arthropods by having a three-segmented body, three pairs of jointed legs and – usually – two pairs of jointed wings. They are the most abundant life form on earth, with millions of species worldwide. At least 26 different orders are recognised, comprising a bewildering variety of families. Among those in the Peruvian Andes are the springtails (Collembola), earwigs (Dermaptera), mantids and cockroaches (Dictyoptera), mayflies (Ephemeroptera), termites (Isoptera), lacewings and ant-lions (Neuroptera) and stick insects (Phasmida). However a number of other insect orders have been better studied, and we describe some of these in more detail here.

BUGS AND BEETLES

The term 'bug' is often used generally to mean an insect of some sort, especially beetles. Scientifically speaking, however, the order Hemiptera comprises the 'true' bugs. These include many groups of insects that are very familiar to most people: aphids, shield bugs, assassin bugs, cicadas, scale insects, plant lice and leafhoppers, to name a few. The name Hemiptera means 'half-winged' and refers to the *partially* hardened front pair of wings found in each species. This may account for the common confusion with beetles. Beetles belong to a separate order called Coleoptera, meaning 'sheath-winged'. Their front pairs of wings are *totally* hardened, forming protective cases (called elytra) over their flight wings.

Despite their apparent similarities, bugs and beetles are very different. Bugs develop as nymphs, which grow in size but always resemble their adult form. Beetles develop from caterpillar-like larvae called grubs, which then pupate and eventually turn into adults. Another fundamental difference between the two groups is in their methods of feeding. Bugs have piercing and sucking mouthparts, with which they feed on fluids, such as sap, nectar, blood and the innards of other insects. Beetles, by contrast, have jaws for chewing, with which they feed on a huge variety of both plant and animal matter. This means that the two groups of insects occupy different niches in the many different High Andean ecosystems they occupy. Beetles are also a favourite food of many Andean mammals, including the spectacled bear.

Beetles

Beetles make up the largest order of insects around the world, and many families are found in the Peruvian Andes. Montane tiger beetles (Cicindelidae) of the genus *Pseudoxycheila* are conspicuous inhabitants of many montane forest habitats. These terrestrial beetles hunt smaller invertebrates with great speed, and are often encountered basking in the sunshine on bare ground. The rather oddly named pleasing fungus beetles (Erotylidae) are easy to find in many Peruvian cloud forest habitats due to their bright colours, slow flight and distinctive hump-backed appearance.

The bright colours are actually a warning to predators. When threatened, the adults secrete a noxious fluid from their legs and anus. Pleasing fungus beetles are often found on the undersides of bracket fungi that grow on dead, fallen trees.

Other beetle families found in the Peruvian Andes include the longhorn beetles (Cerambycidae). These are wood-boring beetles with extremely long antennae and their body colours blend in with the lichen- or moss-covered tree trunks on which they forage. Some of the larger longhorn species even have tiny Pseudoscorpions (order Pseudoscorpionida) living underneath their wing coverts, where they feed on harmful mites. Andean ladybirds (Coccinelidae) belonging to the genus *Eriopis* or *Hippodamia* can often be found sheltering in the high altitude, alpine-like cushion plants. Click beetles (Elateridae) vary greatly in colour, and have slender bodies and normally a distinctive point at the start of the thorax. Their name derives from the distinct noise they make when flipping themselves over if they land on their backs.

DUNG BEETLES: AN ECOLOGICAL ROLE

Dung beetles (Scarabaeidae) have been studied in some depth by many entomologists. Some 25 genera, comprising hundreds of species, have been recorded in the Peruvian Andes. These sturdy insects play an important role in montane ecosystems by dispersing seeds and recycling nutrients. They rapidly bury vertebrate dung and roll away balls of it with their back legs. This has given rise to their other common name, 'tumble bugs'. Dung beetles also breed in dung pats, for which competition between individuals and different species is often very intense. Unlike dung beetles of temperate forests, however, competition between tropical montane dung beetles is restricted to the adults. By concealing their dung balls, most Andean dung beetles ensure that their larvae are not exposed to competition.

Dung beetles are highly susceptible to deforestation of montane habitats. Smaller forest patches contain fewer species and lower population levels. In severely deforested areas of the Andes, dung beetles are unable to perform their ecological services, and levels of dung burial are greatly reduced. This disrupts plant seed dispersal and nutrient cycling, and may have important long-term consequences for plant regeneration and montane forest dynamics.

Bugs

Compared with beetles, relatively few true bug families have, so far, been recorded in the Peruvian Andes. Treehoppers (Membracidae) are among the most varied and bizarre-shaped insects in the region. In most species, the area immediately behind the head has evolved an elaborate curved design, allowing some species to mimic thorns and other parts of plants. The Reduviidae is a family of highly predatory bugs that includes the blood-sucking kissing bugs, or conenoses (*Triotoma* spp.), and the assassin bugs. These can present a hazard to humans, as some species feed on blood and act as vectors for Chagas' disease, a long-term disorder which can bring about premature senility and, ultimately, death. Charles Darwin is widely believed to have returned to Britain with this disease after his travels to South America on the *Beagle*. The scale insect *Dactylopius coccus* lives on prickly pear cacti (*Opuntia* spp.), feeding on their moisture and nutrients. The species is also known as the cochineal insect. It produces a substance known as carminic acid to deter predators, which is traditionally harvested by people to use as a dye. First the insects are cultivated on cacti. Then the eggs and females are harvested, dried and crushed to yield the acid that makes the dye. Recently, however, synthetic substitutes have reduced the market for natural cochineal.

Cochineal insect activity on a prickly pear cactus (TM/SAP)

BUTTERFLIES AND MOTHS

Among the most familiar and attractive insects are the butterflies and moths, which together comprise the order Lepidoptera. The name translates as 'scaled-wings', which refers to the mosaics of tiny overlapping scales, like roof tiles, that make up their four patterned wings. These scales also cover the body and limbs of the insects. The prevailing view is that the ancestral species evolved these scales as a means of protection, because they easily come loose, making the creatures 'slippery' to touch: birds' bills and spiders' webs are often left dusted with butterfly scales as their intended target makes good its getaway. Scales have since evolved many other functions, including identification, camouflage, warning colouration and mimicry. The incredible diversity in wing colouration, along with the variety in distinctive flight patterns, has made butterfly watching an increasingly popular hobby in Peru.

In some countries no real distinction is made between butterflies and moths, but there are some diagnostic details that separate the two. Generally speaking, moths are nocturnal and butterflies are diurnal – although some moths are active by day. Moths tend to be cryptically coloured, while butterflies are more striking, although again there are exceptions. Another useful tip is to examine the antennae. Those of butterflies end in a definite 'club' shape, while those of moths can be wiry, feathered or tapered, but never clubbed. Butterflies are also able to close their wings together above their backs, rather like the pages of a book. Moths cannot close their wings in this way, always having to hold them open or fold them flat over their bodies.

Both butterflies and moths have caterpillars as their larvae, which generally feed on foliage and other plant matter. These turn into pupae, called chrysalises. Moth chrysalises are surrounded by cocoons, above or below ground, whereas butterfly chrysalises are suspended in sheltered places in the open. When the adults (imagos) emerge, they climb to perches where they can expand and dry their wings without any risk of harm.

Butterflies

Many Andean butterflies have evolved behavioural adaptations to their montane environment. These species tend not to fly very far and seek immediate cover when conditions get too windy, otherwise their colonies would become so scattered that individuals would have difficulty meeting and reproducing. Consequently, small colonies manage to eke out an existence in seemingly unlikely places. Relatively few species can survive the rigours of these high altitude environments, but some families are well represented – particularly among the skippers (Hesperiidae); blues, coppers and hairstreaks (Lycaenidae); vanessids (Nymphalinae); whites and sulphurs (Pieridae); and browns and satyrs (Satyrinae). One of the more striking species is *Morpho sulkowski*, a very large highland representative of the *Morpho* genus, with dazzling blue upperwings and beige underwings.

Top The sulphur butterfly (*Colias euxanthe*) is common at high altitudes. (JSP)
Above You can distinguish diurnal moths from butterflies by their habit of resting with open wings. (HA/MV)

Moths

In montane forest habitats of 2,000–3,000m, the most common moths belong to the family Sphingidae. These are more commonly known as hawk moths, sphinx moths and hornworms. Most are moderate to large in size, and are easily distinguished from other species by their streamlined bodies, narrow, triangular-shaped wings, and rapid, sustained flight. The reference to a sphinx comes from the classic pose adopted by the caterpillars when threatened. Hawk moths hover in mid-air whilst feeding on nectar from flowers, an ability that they share with only a few other insects, such as hoverflies, as well as hummingbirds and certain bats.

Also common at these elevations are members of the genus *Amastus* (family Arctiidae) – more commonly known as tiger moths or wasp moths, because of their remarkable resemblance to their namesakes. Wasp moths not only mimic the appearance of wasps or bees, but also their flight patterns. Much rarer species, such as the Andean silkmoth (*Bathyphlebia aglia*) and the mountain tailed moth (*Janoides bethulia*) are only found in the cloud and elfin forests of the Cordillera Vilcabamba in southern Peru, and similar habitats in central Peru.

In the barren, higher elevations of the altiplano (over 4,000m), moths require a number of adaptations to survive the harsh conditions. Certain noctuid winter moths have a circulatory system that includes a special 'counter-current heat exchanger' in their bodies to cope with extreme cold temperatures (the moths 'recycle' body heat in their thorax and prevent it from flowing to the head or abdomen). They are also insulated by a coat of dense, hair-like scales.

Entomologists currently estimate there to be more than 4,200 butterfly species in Peru, and likely to be several times that number of moths. Although there are fewer species in the Andes than in the lowland rainforests, they still number in the hundreds. Species new to science are being discovered annually. Undoubtedly, one of the best locations for Andean butterflies is the cloud forest habitats around Machu Picchu, with over 252 species to be found.

FLIES

Many winged insects are described as flies of one sort or another, but the 'true' flies (Diptera) are distinguished by having just one pair of wings. The other pair has been reduced to tiny club-shaped organs, called 'halteres', which are responsible for flight balance and co-ordination. This arrangement provides flies with a level of aerial manoeuvrability beyond that of other insects. It is demonstrated best by the hoverflies (Syrphidae), which can also fly backwards and upside down, and execute the most complex aerobatics.

Flies that have a predilection for human blood are described as being 'anthropophilic' (human-loving). Although larger bloodsuckers, such as horse and deer flies (genera *Chrysops, Haematopota, Lepiselaga* and *Tabanus*) can deliver painful bites, the species that cause the most nuisance are the biting black flies (genus *Simulium*) and biting midges (genera *Culicoides* and *Leptoconops*). This is because they attack en masse and are so small – often referred to as 'no-see-ums' – that they are almost impossible to fend off. One species, common at Machu Picchu, is known in Quechua as *pumahuacachi*: 'the fly that makes the puma cry!'

ANTS, BEES, WASPS AND SAWFLIES

True flies are most likely to be confused with members of the order Hymenoptera, which contains the ants, bees, wasps and sawflies, not least because many true flies gain protection from predators by mimicking bees and wasps. The Hymenoptera are one of the largest groups of insects, and many species are often referred to as 'eusocial insects' because they live socially, with different castes performing different tasks within the nest. Undeveloped or neutered females are particularly important members of the community, as workers for toiling and soldiers for defence. There are also queens (sexually developed females) and drones (sexually developed males) responsible for reproduction. Other Hymenopterans have evolved solitary, parasitic (using other species to rear their brood) or parasitoid (with larvae that live within other species) lifestyles.

Bees

Most Andean bee species occur in the cloud forest, and only a few species, such as the stingless bees (Apidae) can thrive in the higher altitudes of the paramo and puna. As a result, pollination at these higher elevations is mainly carried out by true flies or butterflies. Many Andean Hymenopterans have to cope with large, daily changes in weather conditions, which can have a serious effect on their flight and foraging activity. In fact, many Andean plants have prolonged flower longevity – a strategy that may have evolved to increase their chances of pollination.

The Peruvian black bumblebee (*Bombus atratus*) can often be found around disturbed cloud forest habitats at above 2,000m. Its nests are active year-round, and can contain up to eight active queens and more than 80 workers. The Andean flower bee (*Anthophora walteri*) nests in flat ground or small banks in semi-arid montane habitats. Several species of sand or digger wasps (genus *Ammophila*) inhabit the paramo and puna. These wasps paralyse caterpillars and inter them in excavated tunnels as sources of fresh food for their larvae.

Ants

Ants are omnipresent in many Andean ecosystems. The field Inca-ant (*Camponotus inca*) can be found underneath boulders in the puna around Lake Titicaca. This species has a rather unusual symbiotic (mutually beneficial) relationship with the puna ground spider (*Eilico puno*). The spider lives amongst the ants, which it closely resembles, and lays its egg sacs in their colonies. When the egg sacs are exposed or threatened, the adult ants carry them into underground portions of their nest. In return, the ground spider shares some of its food with the ant colony. Other common ant species of the region include the red Inca-ant (*Carebara inca*), the Peruvian ant (*Acanthoponera peruviana*) and the Andean ant (*Gnamptogenys andina*).

MANUFACTURING MOUNTAIN FRAGRANCE

Orchid bees, also known as Euglossine bees, are closely related to bumblebees and honey bees (family Apidae). There are many species, often embellished with dazzling iridescent, metallic colours – mainly green, blue or purple. This has resulted in other common names, such as gold bees, emerald bees or jewel bees. Unlike bumblebees, however, most species of the Peruvian Andes are solitary. Male orchid bees have specially modified legs, with which they collect and store many different, volatile chemicals from orchid flowers. The males are known to travel tens of kilometres to find specific orchid species from which to collect these essential oils. The males scrape off the chemicals from the orchids using specially adapted front legs, and then transfer them to an expanded section on their hind legs as they hover. These chemicals are then metabolised by the males and used to attract females, who inevitably select the males with the most diverse selection of perfumes.

DRAGONFLIES AND DAMSELFLIES

Among the most striking insects of the Peruvian Andes are the dragonflies and damselflies. These common diurnal insects are most often found near water. The name of their order, Odonata, translates as 'toothed-ones' in allusion to their powerful predatory jaws. Dragonflies are strong flyers, patrolling the skies for prey, such as other airborne insects, which they catch and eat on the wing. Damselflies have a weaker flight, and tend to remain within their riparian habitat, feeding on other weak-flying insects such as mosquitoes and mayflies. At rest, dragonflies hold their wings out flat, while damselflies typically fold them over their backs (though flat-wing damselflies are the exception to this rule). The larvae of both dragonflies and damselflies are ferocious aquatic predators.

Top Orchid bee (NT)
Above Hawker dragonfly (JP)

The most impressive and conspicuous species are the hawker dragonflies (Aeshnidae). These large insects patrol back and forth along clearings, like miniature biplanes on reconnaissance missions. They often display predominantly blue-on-black body markings, which has given rise to another common name – blue darners (darning needles). Hawker dragonflies can be found at several Andean locations, including the muddy, open areas around Huacarpay Lakes, and around the ruins of Sacsayhuaman, both near Cusco. Club-tail dragonflies (Gomphidae) are around 40–70mm in length, and some species, such as those of the genus *Phyllogomphoides*, are easily recognised by the 'lump' on the end of the tail that resembles a club, and the yellow-on-black body markings. Emerald dragonflies, such as *Gomphomacromia fallax*, and skimmer dragonflies, such as *Brechmorhoga rapax*, are readily found in the cloud forest above 2,500m.

The cloud forest around Aguas Calientes and Machu Picchu is a good habitat for banner-wing damselflies (Polythoridae), such as the stunning electric-blue banner-wing (*Cora terminalis*). Numerous species of flat-wing damselfly (Megapodagrionidae) and pond damselfly (Coenagrionidae) can be found along the larger Andean rivers, such as the Rio Urubamba, in southern Peru.

GRASSHOPPERS AND CRICKETS

All grasshoppers and crickets have two pairs of wings. The name of their order, Orthoptera, means 'straight-winged' – so-called because their forewings are modified into stiffened covers for protecting the membranous, fan-like, hind wings. All Orthopterans have modified hind legs for jumping, and many species communicate by stridulating or 'singing'. The noise is achieved in a similar way to running one's thumbnail along the teeth of a comb. Grasshoppers rub a leg against a wing, while crickets rub both wings together. Songs are species-specific, and crickets have two types of song: a calling song and a courting song. The calling song attracts females and repels other males, and is fairly loud. When a female approaches, the male will then use a much quieter courting song to conclude his performance.

The classification of grasshoppers and crickets is complicated, but as a general rule grasshoppers are folivorous (leaf-eating), while crickets are omnivorous (eating both vegetable and animal matter). In the Peruvian Andes, Orthopterans reach their highest levels of diversity and abundance in the cloud and elfin forests on the eastern slopes. Predominant here are the grasshoppers and locusts (Acrididae). True crickets (Gryllidae) are often confused with grasshoppers because of their similar body structure and jumping hind legs, but they are easily distinguished by their more flattened bodies and extremely long antennae. Ground-hoppers (Tetrigidae) are also known as pygmy grasshoppers, and include some of the smallest montane Orthopteran species. Pygmy mole crickets (Tridactylidae) are often found alongside montane streams and ponds. These small, active jumpers

Leaf katydids are masters of disguise. (HP)

have modified legs used for digging burrows in areas with softer, sandy soils, and are unusual in that the males do not sing. Bush crickets or katydids (Tettigoniidae) are also known as long-horned grasshoppers because they have extremely long, thread-like antennae. Despite some species feeding on leaves, flowers and seeds, others are highly predatory, capturing other montane insects, snails and even small lizards.

ARACHNIDS (SPIDERS, SCORPIONS AND ALLIES)

Spiders are arachnids (Arachnea), along with scorpions (Scorpiones), harvestmen (Opiliones), mites and ticks (Acari) and whip-scorpions (Thelyphonidae). This class of arthropods differs from insects by having eight legs, no antennae, and a body divided into two, not three, principal sections. The spider fauna of Peru is large and diverse. Spiders are, however, notoriously difficult to identify with certainty because they often differ in only microscopic characteristics. In addition, there is a great deal of variation within single species, and immature spiders can look quite different from adults. Spiders are highly predatory. All species produce silk from structures called spinnerets at the tip of their abdomen. The silk is a thin, high-tensile protein strand used to trap insects in a variety of strategies. Some spiders also use it to build egg sacs, wrap and preserve prey, and line their burrows. Andean spiders employ a wonderful variety of disguises with which to ambush prey and provide protection from predators. The majority kill their prey by injecting venom, which also helps to liquefy the prey for consumption.

SPIDERS

Spider imagery occurs in Peruvian art from the middle of the first millennium BC, suggesting that spiders played a role in early Andean mythology (the spider's ability to catch and kill live prey has often been associated with sacrifice, whilst other sources suggest that from the 16th century, the Inca associated spiders with rainfall and fertility). Spiders were also a common feature on golden, ornamental jewellery, such as nose rings, discovered in the northern Peruvian Andes and dating from around the second half of the first millennium AD

At the highest elevations, in wetter altiplano habitat and Andean marshes at over 4,000m, numerous money spiders (*Linyphiid* spp.), can be found living underneath cushion plants. At lower elevations, wandering spiders (Ctenidae) – socalled because they meander around at night hunting for insects – can be found in nearly every nook and cranny in cloud forest habitats. Wolf spiders (Lycosidae) are similarly named after their method of hunting. These spiders are highly robust, nocturnal hunters of Andean forests, and run down their prey using a combination of agility and good eyesight. The family Therasophidae contains the terrestrial Neotropical tarantulas, some of which are also called bird-eating spiders. Species such as the large Andean striped bird-eater (*Lasiodora striatus*) are becoming popular as pets because they are fairly hardy and not aggressive. Closely related to the tarantulas are the funnel-web spiders (Agelenidae) and the trap-door spiders (Ctenizidae), both medium-sized spiders that are named after the ingenious ways in which they catch their prey. Trap-door spiders construct burrows that are capped with a 'trap-door', constructed from their silk and heavily camouflaged with soil particles. It is hinged on one side and the spider holds onto the underside. When prey ventures too close, the spider lunges out of the half-open door to capture it. The orb-weavers (Araneidae) constitute one of the largest families of spiders in the Andes. These are the species that build 'normal' flat webs with sticky spiral capture silk.

SCORPIONS

Scorpions also have eight legs, and their bodies are divided into two segments. The cephalothrorax is home to the scorpions' eyes, mouth parts, claws or pedipalps, and four pairs of walking legs. The abdomen contains the sexual organs, a tough, protective cuticle, and the characteristic tail, bearing the sting, or telson. All scorpion species possess venom, which is neurotoxic (the venom interferes with the prey's nervous system). However, scorpion venom is designed for action upon their prey (eg: other invertebrates) and most scorpions are relatively harmless to humans. Scorpions are also viviparous – they give birth to live young that are then carried on the mother's back.

In the more arid, high-altitude habitats, a number of smaller scorpions can be found by turning over stones or investigating cracks, crevices, small burrows and rocky outcrops. These include the black highland pit scorpion (*Orobothriurus alticola*), Andean scorpion (*Brachistosternus andinus*), Inca scorpion (*Pachakutej inca*) – named after the Inca Pachacutec – and dusky mountain scorpion (*Zabius fuscus*), which can reach a length of about 6cm.

Andean scorpion (TM/SAP)

ANDEAN
HOT-SPOTS

Cordillera Blança (HB)

SEVEN OF THE BEST *with David Hilton*

The Peruvian Andes offer a wide variety of landscapes in which to enjoy wildlife. From the damp cloud forests of the eastern slopes, to the desert-like altiplano, lush inter-montane valleys, rolling puna grasslands, elfin forest, high Andean woodlands, and dry western slopes all provide a home for a multitude of creatures. Amid this vast region, a number of sites are more accessible than others, and some are especially rewarding for visitors. This chapter gives a brief overview of seven popular places.

CUSCO AND THE SACRED VALLEY OF THE INCAS

As the ancient epicentre of the vast Inca empire, the beautiful historic city of Cusco is the regional base for any tourist, and in the town centre it has managed to retain much of its old colonial charm. The nearby Sacred Valley of the Incas, or Urubamba Valley, provides the trekker with a number of easily accessible day hikes to impressive ruins and wonderful scenery, which means the day can begin and end at your hotel in Cusco. Whilst many tour companies visit the area, independent travellers can also easily get away from the crowds and enjoy the wildlife and landscapes on their own terms.

Habitat, climate and terrain

Cusco experiences a refreshing Andean climate, with cool nights and hot days. The surrounding hills are covered by terraced, grassy terrain, with some xerophytic scrub, native *queuna* trees and non-native eucalyptus trees. The Urubamba Valley is warm and pleasant, and significantly milder than Cusco. Sided by high, craggy peaks, the slopes roll down to a lush valley floor, cultivated with maize and other crops.

Key species

Flora: Kiwicha and quinua (Amaranthaceae), agaves or maguey (*Agave americana* and *Furcrea andina*), prickly pear cactus or tuna (*Opuntia* sp.), pepper tree or molle (*Schinus molle*), tree tobacco (*Nictotania glauca*).
Terrestrial Animals: Culpeo or South American fox, wild cavy or montane guinea pig, white-tailed deer, pampas cat, white-eared opossum, marcapata false coral snake.
Birds: Andean flicker, Andean gull, Andean swift, giant humingbird, bearded mountaineer, chestnut-breasted mountain finch, band-tailed seedeater, Peruvian sierra finch, bare-faced ground-dove

Visitor information

Location: Cusco (3,360m) is nestled at the head of the Watanay Valley, in the eastern fringes of Peru's southern Andes. The Sacred Valley lies approximately 20km to the northeast, at an average altitude of 2,850m.
When to visit: The drier winter months of May–September provide clear, rainless days and colder nights. At other times it is warmer, but frequent rains make for wet and muddy hiking.
Traveller's tips: Take two or three days to acclimatise and explore the valley. Consider purchasing the Boleto Turístico in Cusco and a tourist map if you plan to visit several ruins in the area.

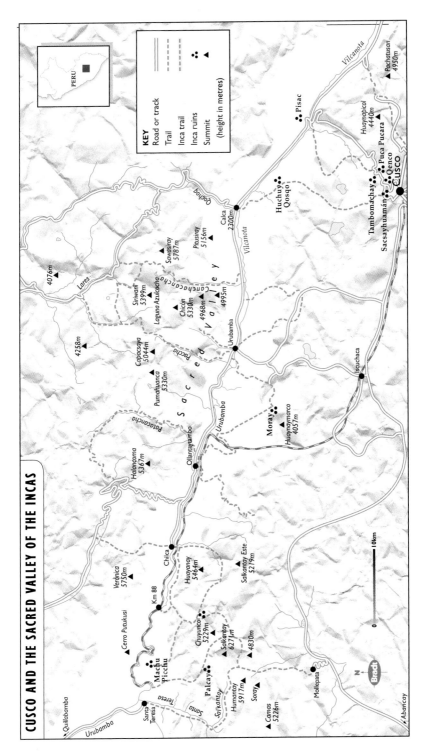

CUSCO AND THE SACRED VALLEY OF THE INCAS

KEY
Road or track
Trail
Inca trail
Inca ruins
Summit
(height in metres)

PERU

Vilcanota
Pachatusan 4950m
Huaynapical 4440m
Puca Pucara
Qenco
CUSCO
Tambomachay
Sacsayhuamán
Huchuy Qosqo
Pisac
Calca 2300m
Vilcanota
Qochoq
Pitusiray 5156m
Sawasiray 5787m
Sirwani 5399m
Laguna Azulcocha
Chicón 5330m
4968m
Canchacancha
4995m
Urubamba
Sacred Valley
407m
Lares
4258m
Capacsaya 5044m
Paccha
Pumahuanca 5330m
Patacancha
Ollantaytambo
Urubamba
Moray
Huaynaymarco 4057m
Itsuchaca
Halancoma 5367m
Verónica 5750m
Chilca
Km 88
Cerro Putukusi
Machu Picchu
Huayanay 5464m
Salkantay Este 5219m
Chuyunco 5229m
Salkantay 6271m
4830m
Palcay
Humantay 5917m
Soray
Camas 5226m
Mollepata
Santa Teresa
Santa Teresa
Salkantay
Quillabamba
Urubamba
Abancay

N
Bradt

0   10km

Machu Picchu (HB)

THE MACHU PICCHU HISTORICAL SANCTUARY

The Inca citadel of Machu Picchu is undoubtedly Peru's most famous tourist attraction, although the hitherto little-known ruins of Choquequirao and coastal ruins of the pre-Inca cultures in the northwest are gaining fame rapidly. Despite its omnipresent tourists, Machu Picchu remains awe-inspiring. The Machu Picchu Historical Sanctuary (MPHS) is a UNESCO World Heritage Site, recognised for its outstanding cultural and natural beauty, and renowned for its high levels of endemism and biodiversity.

Habitat, climate and terrain

The ruins experience relatively warm and humid conditions due to the sheltering effect of the surrounding mountains, and are set in high-level cloud forest. The sanctuary, covering 32,592ha, encompasses a variety of habitats, from montane, cloud and elfin forest to puna at the higher altitudes. This range of ecosystems is responsible for a wide diversity of plants and more than 400 species of bird, and is renowned for its numerous endemic and near-endemic species.

Key species

Flora: Bee orchids (*Ophrys* sp.), tillandsia bromeliads (*Tillslandsia* sp.), pisonay (*Erythrina edulis*), Inca orchid (*Sobralia dichotoma*), wiñyawanya (*Epidendrum secundum*), bat's face orchid (*Prosthechea vespa*), dragon's face orchid (*Prosthechea fusca*).

Terrestrial Animals: Spectacled (Andean) bear, South American coati, Neotropical otter, cusco chinchilla rat, white-eared opossum.

Birds: Inca wren, Andean condor, torrent duck, white-capped dipper, white-tipped swift, tricolored brush-finch, rusty flowerpiercer, white-winged black-tyrant, black-chested buzzard-eagle.

Visitor information

Location: The ruins sit astride a prominent ridge at 2,040m, overlooking the meandering Urubamba Valley. The nearest modern settlement to the site is the shanty town of Aguas Calientes, which has plenty of accommodation to suit all budgets.

When to visit: May–September are the drier months, with great views possible until December, when the rains begin in earnest. August can be hazy, when local farmers habitually burn off grass and other vegetation.

Traveller's tips: Arrive at daybreak for the best views of both the ruins and the wildlife. The 06.00 bus from Aguas Calientes can be booked through some tour companies. Hiking back to Aguas Calientes, rather than taking the bus, allows you to see a variety of birdlife.

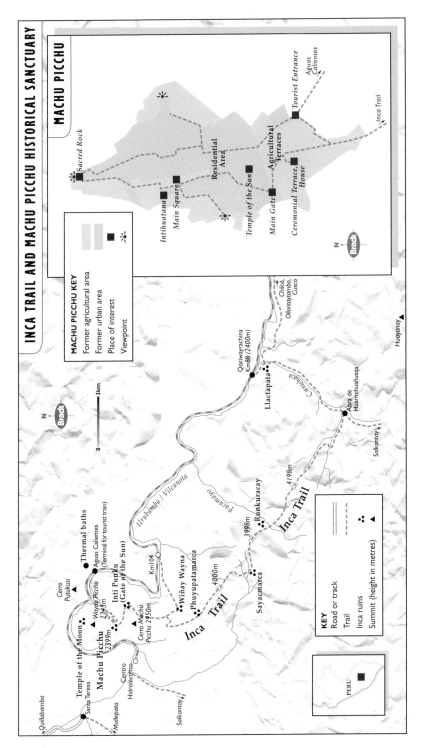

INCA TRAIL AND MACHU PICCHU HISTORICAL SANCTUARY

MACHU PICCHU

MACHU PICCHU KEY

Former agricultural area
Former urban area
Place of interest
Viewpoint

Sacred Rock
Intihuatana
Main Square
Residential Area
Temple of the Sun
Main Gate
Agricultural Terraces
Ceremonial Terrace, House
Tourist Entrance
Aguas Calientes
Inca Trail

N
Bradt

KEY

Road or track
Trail
Inca ruins
Summit (height in metres)

PERU

Quillabamba
Temple of the Moon
Cerro Patukusi
Cerro Patukusi 2743m
Wayna Picchu
Inti Punku (Gate of the Sun)
Machu Picchu 2399m
Cerro Machu Picchu 2950m
Santa Teresa
Mollepata
Centro Hidroléctrico
Salkantay
Thermal baths
Aguas Calientes (Terminal for tourist train)
Km104
Urubamba / Vilcanota
Wiñay Wayna
Phuyupatamarca
4000m
Inca Trail
Sayacmarca
3998m
Runkuracay
Pacaymayo
4198m
Inca Trail
Abra de Huarmihuañusqa
Salkantay
Castellaca
Qoriwayrachina Km88 (2400m)
Llactapata
Chilca, Ollantaytambo, Cusco
Huayanay

0 3km
N
Bradt

Climbing to Warmaywanusca Pass along the Inca Trail (HP)

THE INCA TRAIL AND CORDILLERA VILCABAMBA

This extraordinary region is full of wonders for the traveller. A plethora of Inca ruins, majestic high peaks, and great flora and fauna, make this one of the most popular trekking areas in Latin America. Perhaps the most famous trek in the world, the Inca Trail is a superb way to experience the region's cultural marvels, whilst other areas are generally better for wildlife spotting – including the cloudforests near Choquequirao. The trek from Huncacalle to Choquequirao is a spectacular week-long journey.

Habitat, climate and terrain

This mountain range consists of cloud forest, elfin forest, and tough puna bunchgrass smothering the higher reaches. The Inca Trail passes through each of these diverse ecosystems. Birds such as the Andean condor and grey-breasted mountain-toucan find refuge here. The climate is mild and stable, with warm days and cool nights, varying slightly with altitude.

Key species

Flora: Antuta (*Cantua buxifolia*), Spanish broom or retama (*Spartium junecum*), snail orchids (*Cochlioda* sp.), potato (*Solanum tuberosum*).

Terrestrial Animals: Spectacled (Andean) bear, puma, South American fox or culpeo, mountain viscacha, cusco spectacled lizard.

Birds: Cuzco brush finch, grey-breasted mountain toucan, Vilcabamba tapaculo, creamy-crested spimetail, red-crested cotinga, scarlet-bellied mountain tanager, white-collared jay, undulated antpitta.

Visitor information

Location: Stretching to the west of Cusco, the Cordillera Vilcabamba is sandwiched between the two great rivers, Apurimaci and Urubamba. The Inca Trail begins approximately halfway between Ollantaytambo and Aguas Calientes, at the 'Km 88' railway station.

When to visit: May–October is generally dry, providing more comfortable trekking and camping conditions, though the trail can be very crowded.

Traveller's tips: The Inca Trail is now strictly regulated and can be hiked with only licensed agencies and guides. Trekking permits are limited and must be booked in advance. There are latrine facilities at all campsites and all rubbish must be packed away. Early starts allow you to see more wildlife and fewer tourists. If you want to explore the mountains on your own, there are no such restrictions on other trails.

CORDILLERA VILCANOTA

This vast cordillera, the highest in southern Peru, sees fewer visitors than the adjacent Vilcabamba range, but is becoming more popular as trekking permits for the Inca Trail become more limited. It is a remote high-altitude wilderness, with huge glaciers, magnificent mountain scenery, thermal springs and locals who still practise their traditional way of life. Large patches of *Polylepis* forest harbour rare wildlife, including the critically endangered bird, the royal cinclodes.

Habitat, climate and terrain

Tough puna vegetation dominates the desolate plains, supporting large communities of llamas and alpacas. This austere landscape is punctuated by glacial lakes, fed by melting glaciers beneath snowy peaks. Sheltered valleys still contain relict patches of *Polylepis* woodland. The high-altitude climate produces high levels of ultraviolet light during the clear days, followed by freezing cold temperatures at night due to a lack of cloud cover. The chilly wind can be incessant.

Key species

Flora: Warqu (*Opuntia flocossa*), gynoxys tree (*Gynoxys oleifola*), sauco tree (*Sambucus peruviana*), lupin bush (*Lupinus mutabillis*), Qeuna *Polylepis* sp.
Terrestrial animals: White-tailed deer, Molina's hog-nosed skunk, long-tailed weasel, mountain viscacha, hairy long-nosed armadillo.
Birds: Royal cinclodes, giant conebill, white-browed tit-spinetail, ash-breasted tit-tyrant, line-fronted canastero, tawny tit-spinetail.

Visitor information

Location: Located south and east of Cusco, and extending for 200km, the range runs parallel to the eastern side of the Sacred Valley of the Incas and the Cusco–Puno road and railway line. Large areas are over 3,000m in altitude.
When to visit: Very little rain falls from May–October, resulting in hot, sunny days. Rains begin in October, with the wettest and least windy months being January and February.
Traveller's tips: You will need several days in order to appreciate this great wilderness area. It is advisable to acclimatise to the high altitude before you start trekking.

Cordillera Vilcanota (HB)

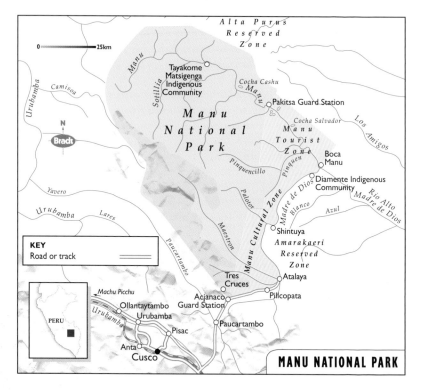

MANU NATIONAL PARK

MANU NATIONAL PARK (ANDEAN SECTION)

The vast Manu National Park covers a total area of 1,881,200ha, and ranges in altitude from 365m (Manu River mouth) to 4,000m (Cerro Huascar). It is located on the eastern slopes of the Andes, and extends down from precipitous mountains into the Amazon River basin, protecting almost the entire watershed of the River Manu. Much of the park consists of lowland rainforest and as such lies beyond the scope of this book. Nonetheless the park also protects large areas of high-altitude habitat, which are of particular interest to visitors to the Peruvian Andes.

Habitat, climate and terrain

Manu National Park is probably the most biologically diverse protected area in the world. It contains nearly all the ecological formations of eastern Peru, including tropical lowland forest, montane forest and puna grasslands, with their respective flora and fauna. Some botanists claim that Manu has more plant species than any other protected area on the earth: 1,147 have been identified in the park within quite a small area and it is likely that the total number is much higher. A total of more than 1,000 birds have also been identified, including six species of macaw. Among other wildlife highlights of the lowlands are emperor tamarin (*Saguinus imperator*), giant otter (*Pteronura brasiliensis*), jaguar (*Panthera onca*) and black caiman (*Melanosuchus niger*). Climates range from those of the cold, dry Andes to the hot, humid Amazon forests, with colder temperatures and less rainfall at higher altitudes, and year-round fog in montane forest regions.

Key species

Flora: Alder (*Alnus* sp.), Guzmania bromeliads, Chusquea bamboo (*Chusquea* sp.), Chacpa (*Oreocalis grandiflora*), Chachacomo (*Escallonia resinosa*).

Terrestrial animals: Common woolly monkey, dwarf brocket deer, northern pudu, mountain paca, mussurana snake, puma.

Birds: Red and white antpitta, marcapata spinetail, puma thistletail, streaked tuftedcheek, pearled treerunner, Azara's spinetail, Peruvian treehunter.

Visitor information

Location: The park lies in the provinces of Manu and Paucartambo (departments of Madre de Dios and Cuzco respectively), comprising lands on the eastern slopes of the Andes and on the Peruvian Amazones.

When to visit: May–November during the austral winter is best as it is the dry season.

Traveller's tips: Take an organised tour with specialist guides.

Montane forest in Manu National Park (TM/SAP)

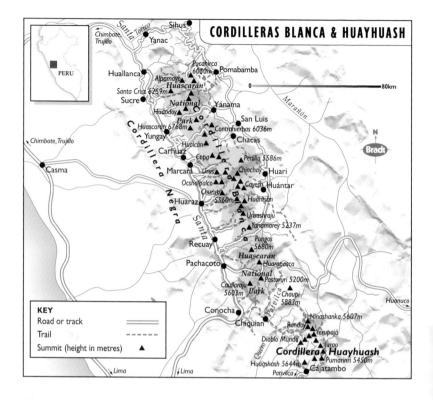

CORDILLERAS BLANCA AND HUAYHUASH

The Cordillera Blanca is the highest tropical mountain range on earth, and is regarded as South America's Mecca for high-altitude climbing and trekking. The nearby Cordillera Huayhuash has remained one of Peru's most remote highland territories. The Huascarán National Park protects many of the rare species living within the Cordillera Blanca.

Habitat, climate and terrain

Within the Cordillera Blanca, snowy mountains tower over undulating, rocky terrain, which leads down to sloping puna and tight valleys harbouring *Polylepis* forests. Lower still, terraced fields are interspersed among tough *ichu* grass-covered slopes. The Cordillera Negra, on the western side of the river Santa, is dry and snowless. The climate is typically Andean, with warm, often windy, days and cold nights. It can be very windy in the narrow valleys of the Cordillera Blanca. The Cordillera Huayhuash has large expanses of rolling puna, dramatic glaciers and massive rock faces. There are many glacial lakes in both ranges.

Key species

Flora: Wamanripa (*Senecio tephrosiode*), roseton (*Stangea henricii*), *Puya raimondii*, woolly cacti or old men cacti (*Oreocereus* sp.), chinguirito (*Baccaris genistelloide*).

Terrestrial animals: Andean huemal, mountain viscacha, Andean mountain cat, Peruvian slender snake, puma, white-tailed deer.

Birds: Baron's spinetail, plain-tailed warbling finch, white-cheeked cotinga, giant coot, rufous-eared brush finch, crested duck, stripe-headed antpitta, rainbow starfrontlet.

Visitor information

Location: The Cordillera Blanca extends for 180km along the eastern side of the valley known as the Callejón de Huaylas, in the middle of which sits the town of Huaraz (3,090m). The Cordillera Huayhuash lies to the south, about 100km from Huaraz.

When to visit: The most settled weather is during May–September, with little rain, sunny days and cold, clear nights. Weather is unpredictable for the rest of the year, and heavy rainfall can be expected December–March, although the nights are milder.

Traveller's tips: Certified climbing and trekking guides are available in Huaraz. Independent trekking is also possible and very rewarding. Mules, if required, can generally be organised in the village where the trek begins, and certainly from outfitters in Huaraz.

Cordillera blanca (HB)

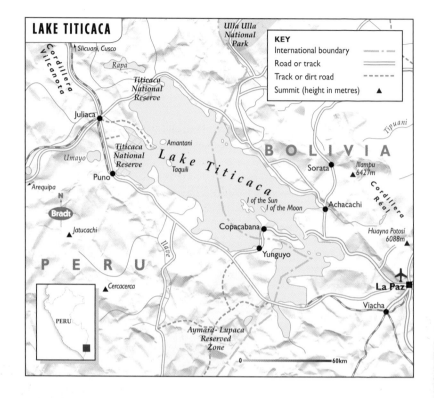

LAKE TITICACA

KEY
- International boundary
- Road or track
- Track or dirt road
- Summit (height in metres) ▲

LAKE TITICACA

As the mythological birth place of the Incas, Lake Titicaca is revered by the locals to this day and is one of the geographical highlights of South America. This, the world's highest navigable lake, resembles the Mediterranean, with its deep blue skies and crystal-clear water. However, the snowy-peaked backdrop of the Cordillera Real is indisputably Andean, as are the local inhabitants. Despite the harshness of the environment, the lake's shores, waters and islands play host to a remarkable array of both natural and cultural heritage.

Habitat, climate and terrain

The altiplano terrain that surrounds the lake is dry, barren and hilly, with vegetation such as the totora reeds confined to the areas around the lakeshore. This unique aquatic environment has given rise to endemic species such as the flightless short-winged grebe and the bizarre-looking Titicaca frog. Its high exposed position gives the region a harsh climate of strong solar radiation during the day and bitterly cold temperatures at night. Winds are frequent, chilly and strong.

Key species

Flora: Wamanripa (*Senecia tephrosiodesis*), totora reeds (*Juncus andicola*), ichu grass (*Stipa ichu*), bush grasses (*Calamagrostis*), bentgrasses (*Agrostis*), bromes (*Bromus*).

Terrestrial animals: Vicuña, greater grison, common yellow-toothed cavy, brown hare, Andean hairy armadillo, Andean lancehead snake, llama and alapca.

Birds: Short-winged grebe, puna ibis, Andean coot, many-coloured rush-tyrant, wren-like rushbird, Andean gull, puna teal, speckled teal, rufous-naped ground-tyrant.

Visitor information

Location: Straddling the border between Peru and Bolivia, the lake is the most popular crossing point between the two countries. It sits at 3,810m and covers an area of 460,000ha.

When to visit: The rainy season lasts from December–March. The summer months of May–September are predominantly dry, with clear skies. Nights are very cold all year round.

Traveller's tips: Visit both sides of the lake. The Peruvian islands of Suasi, Amantani and Taquile are all worth a visit, as are the floating reed islands where the Uros Indians live. The Bolivian side is cheaper and offers more interesting terrain for the trekker, but the Peruvian side is better for observing the lake's flora and fauna.

The serenity of Lake Titicaca at dusk (HP)

The flight of the condor (HP)

WATCHING WILDLIFE

Searching for and watching Andean wildlife is a very different experience from a traditional African safari or a trek through the rainforest. The whereabouts of the wildlife depends on a variety of factors, including time of year, time of day, weather, and availability of food and water. Different animals react to people in different ways, and the effort needed to find them depends on their habitat and the local topography. Luck certainly plays a part, but success also requires patience, a little experience and an appreciation of other people in your group.

A good field guide is indispensable for birdwatching. With mammals, which tend to be nervous of people, you will need to be more patient than with other animal groups. Invertebrates, amphibians and reptiles pose more complex identification problems, and none of these should be handled, except under the supervision of a qualified guide.

Watching wildlife in Peru can be strenuous, so you should plan the day wisely. It is important to start the day early – sometimes very early! The day's activities will generally also finish early, so you will be able to catch up on sleep by taking an early night. Pre-dawn, the hour before the dawn chorus, is a magical acoustic experience in the humid eastern-slope cloud forests, and a great opportunity to see the wildlife change from the night shift to the day shift. Some forest predators are best observed at this time. Bird activity is at its peak during the first few hours after dawn, and many cloud and elfin forest species are highly active – even during periods of light rain and low cloud (so don't run for shelter every time it rains!). Birdwatchers should also be aware of the midday flock phenomenon: a burst of foraging activity by mixed bird flocks that always seems to happen when you are about to have lunch.

In higher-elevation habitats, such as *Polylepis* woodlands and puna, it is extremely cold at pre-dawn and dawn, with temperatures often below zero. There is also a less strident dawn chorus. So the wildlife watcher does not necessarily have to get up early here – though it is a good idea to get close to these locations as early as possible.

In all Andean habitats, stay alert for signs, sounds and smells. Scrutinise prominent features of the landscape – including boulders and ledges, bogs and streams, emergent or isolated trees, flowering cacti, bromeliads and moss-laden branches – for any signs of animal movement (see *Binoculars* below). Fruiting and flowering trees in humid forest habitats are especially worth checking. You could also try carefully turning over rocks or fallen branches in search of invertebrates or fungi. Using a suitable stick, sift gently through leaf litter for larger beetles, small lizards and amphibians. At higher elevations you can explore boulder scree and small boulder fields for alpine plants and high-altitude invertebrates.

Dusk triggers the end of the day shift and a return to the night shift. There is a burst of activity from mammals and birds before the diurnal wildlife finally settles down for the night, and the nocturnal wildlife takes over. This is the best time to see the most elaborate displays of either the lyre-tailed or swallow-tailed nightjars. Night monkeys awake from their roosts of dense vegetation and begin to forage excitedly, often calling from the treetops on a moonlit night. Along the humid forest edges at roadsides listen out for the repetitive calls of various species of screech owl, and enjoy the soothing nocturnal chorus of forest katydids and other invertebrates in the cloud forest. Whether staying at a lodge or campsite, you should grab any opportunity to take a night walk. Bring a sturdy head-torch: this frees your hands to look among the leaves for camouflaged leaf katydids, stick insects and other invertebrates, or singing frogs perched atop small plants aiming to lure mates and warn off rivals.

WHAT TO BRING

Every travel guide is packed with advice about the sort of equipment you will need for the Peruvian Andes, and you should plan your trip well in advance. However, it is worth highlighting some of the basics here.

Binoculars

Essential! Wildlife will be seen from a variety of distances, and often partially hidden by branches or foliage. Binoculars will give you a much more satisfactory view – and will allow you to see much that you would otherwise miss. If you purchase a new pair, make sure to practise using them before your trip, maybe in your local park or nearby countryside. Develop a habit of methodically searching prominent trees and other features of the landscape. Make sure your binoculars have a robust strap (as short as possible) and a rain-guard. Don't rely on borrowing other people's binoculars: this will cost you valuable sightings – and possibly friends!

Binoculars are not cheap and your choice of brand is really a matter of budget. You should consider size, weight and magnification. A mid-range specification, such as 8x42, often makes a good compromise.

Telescope

A telescope is a good asset for the serious wildlife watcher, but takes up luggage space and can be cumbersome to lug around. A smaller spotting scope with a lightweight extendable monopod can be useful for those who want to watch birds and other wildlife on Andean lakes. Having a telescope also opens up new possibilities for photography (see below).

Field guides

A good field guide will help you identify numerous species by sight, and also by their distribution, ecology (habitat preferences etc) and behaviour. There are illustrated field guides for birds, and photographic guides for plants and butterflies. These are widely available online and from bookstores worldwide, while Peruvian field guides are also available in bookstores and airports in Cusco, Arequipa and Lima.

Clothing

Clothes should be loose-fitting, lightweight and breathable. Thermal under layers are advisable, particularly for higher-elevation habitats. Always wear neutral colours, such as greens, browns or dark blues. Bright clothing is easily spotted by wildlife and may cause it to flee. Long-sleeved tops and long trousers offer protection against insect bites and stings, or thorny plants and cacti. Walking boots are essential (something with good ankle support). You will also need a thermal hat and gloves for the colder, higher elevations. Serious high-altitude hiking requires more specialist equipment and proper advice should be taken.

Some other essentials

- Head-torch: more useful than traditional hand-held torches because it frees your hands to use cameras, turn over vegetation, etc.
- Sunblock: remember that skin burns more quickly at high altitudes due to a greater exposure to UV light, even on overcast days.
- Insect repellent: bugs are less of a problem in the Andes than in the Amazonian lowlands, but it's useful to have some form of repellent for the evenings.
- Sunglasses: useful for travelling in vehicles and when hiking through the open altiplano and puna; they also guard against glare from glacial lakes, salt flats and snow peaks.
- Hat: protects against UV rays and reduces eyestrain under strong sunlight; a wide rim will also protect your neck from sunburn without impeding your hearing.
- Full water bottle: wherever you are in the Andes, you will need to drink a lot more than you would at sea level, so it is vital to keep your water bottle filled.
- Small daypack: to pack a lightweight raincoat, water bottle, cameras, field guides, medication, etc.
- First-aid kit: all tour companies should provide their own, but it is sometimes worthwhile doubling up.
- Umbrella: not as silly as it sounds! Many wildlife watchers prefer to use umbrellas.

Blunt-headed tree snake eating frog (HP)

PHOTOGRAPHY

The age of the digital camera is upon us and now everyone can produce extraordinary wildlife photographs with the minimum of effort. However, the responsible ecotourist should remember to watch and enjoy the wildlife in front of them, instead of just scrolling through the snaps on their camera screen! Serious photographers should do their research before setting out. Meanwhile, the following basic checklist may be helpful for beginners.

- Camera: if you purchase a new camera before your trip, make sure you know how it works; bring the manual, just in case.
- Power supply: bring a spare battery, your recharger and an appropriate adapter.
- Digital storage: always remember spare memory cards/sticks.
- Protection: always keep your camera in a protective case or suitable camera bag that can hold everything at once, and do not expose it to moisture; digital sensors are vulnerable to dust, so change lenses only in a sheltered place; use lens-cleaning tissues.

Digiscoping

Birdwatchers and other wildlife watchers have recently taken to the very popular trend of 'digiscoping' – taking photographs through a telescope. This is very straightforward, so long as you have a suitable digital camera and, with a steady hand, can position it comfortably over the eyepiece of the telescope. You then simply focus your viewfinder with the image in the scope. Some telescopes require an adaptor, but many do not. Guides are always generous and will allow any group member to take photos through their scopes once everyone has first had a decent view.

FURTHER READING

PLANTS

Machu Picchu Orchids, Christenson, E.; published PROFONAMPE (2003).
Wild flowers of the Cordillera Blanca, Kolff, H, and Kolff K.; published The Mountain Institute (1997).

Trees and Bushes from the Sacred Valley of the Incas, Cassinelli del Sante, G. (2000).
Field Guide to the Families and Genera of Woody Plants of Northwest South America, Gentry, A. H. and Vasquez, R.; published University of Chicago Press (1993).

Peru as a centre of domestication – tracing the origin of civilisation through the domesticated plants, Cook, O. F.; published *Journal of Heredity* 16: 95–110 (1969).

MAMMALS

The Distribution and Status of Some Peruvian Mammals, Grimwood, I. R.; Special Publication #21 New York Zoological Society, 1968.

Mammals of the Highlands of Southern Peru, Pearson, O. P; published *Bulletin of the Museum of Comparative Zoology*, Harvard Vol. 106 #3, 1951.

Life History of Mountain Viscachas in Peru, Pearson, O. P (1948); published *Journal of Mammology*, December 1948 #4.

Mammals of the Neotropics, Vol. 3: the Central Neotropics (Vol. 3), Eisenberg, J. F. and Redford, K. H; published University of Chicago Press (1999).

Neotropical Rainforest Mammals, a Field Guide (2nd edition), Emmons, L. H.; published University of Chicago Press (1997).

REPTILES

Lizards: Windows to the Evolution of Diversity, Eric Pianka and Laurie J. Vitt; published University of California Press (2003).

The Venomous Reptiles of Latin America, Campbell, J. M. and Lamar, W. W.; published Comstock Pub Association (1989).

OTHER

Mammals and Birds of the Manu Biosphere Reserve, Peru, Bruce D. Patterson, Douglas F. Stotz, Sergio Solari; published Fieldiana #10 2006

A Strategy for Conserving the Biological Diversity of Polylepis Woodlands of the High Andes in Peru and Bolivia, Fjeldså, J. and Kessler, M.; published CTB/NORDECO, Copenhagen (1996).

Las Mariposas de Machu Picchu; Lamas, G.; published PROFONAMPE (2003).

Llamas